# FEASTING ON

# FISH

# FEASTING ON
# FISH

## LOUISE PICKFORD

*Photographs by Gus Filgate*

a Salamander book

**Published by Salamander Books Limited**
**LONDON**

# A Salamander Book

Published by Salamander Books Ltd
129–137 York Way
London N7 9LG
United Kingdom

ISBN 0 86101 761 7

1  3  5  7  9  8  6  4  2

CREDITS

*Managing Editor:* ANNE MCDOWALL
*Copy Editor:* VERONICA SPERLING
*Designer:* PETER BRIDGEWATER
*Photographer:* GUS FILGATE
*Home Economist:* MAXINE CLARK
*Stylist:* JANE McLEISH
*Typesetting:* CHRIS LANAWAY
*Indexer:* ALISON LEACH
*Colour reproduction:*
P & W GRAPHICS PTE. LTD., SINGAPORE

*Printed in Italy*


ACKNOWLEDGMENT
The author and publishers would like to thank
Chalmers & Gray Fishmongers, 67 Notting Hill Gate,
London W11 3JS, for supplying all the fish used for photography.

# CONTENTS

# INTRODUCTION

≈

A great many varieties of exotic fish are appearing in our supermarkets and fishmongers allowing us to become more adventurous with what we cook. Eating fish has great nutritional benefits too – it is a good source of protein (particularly oily fish and shellfish) and many types are low in saturated fats. Cooking times are short for many fish dishes, making fish an ideal choice for today's busy cook.

Whenever possible, shop for, cook and eat fish on the same day. If you really need to shop in advance, scale, gut, wash and dry the fish and wrap it loosely in foil. Store it in the refrigerator overnight, but no longer. When buying fish, ensure that the gills are bright red and moist. The eyes should also be bright and moist; avoid cloudy shrunken eyes. The flesh should be firm without being over springy and a clean fresh smell of the sea should be the only odour. When buying live shellfish, choose those that look the liveliest. Clams and mussel shells should be tightly closed.

*Preparing fish and shellfish*
Scaling, gutting and filleting fish is actually very easy, but most fishmongers will be happy to do this for you if you wish; I always ask mine to scale the fish, and I would advise you to ask your fishmonger to gut the fish for you as well. Make sure you are armed with a very sharp filleting knife.

To fillet round fish, such as salmon, trout and mackerel, remove the head and tail and cut along one side of the backbone from head to tail. Keeping the knife at a slight angle, close to the backbone, work the top fillet away from the bones with a sawing motion. Turn the fish over and repeat with the second fillet.

To fillet flat fish, such as plaice and sole, place the fish onto a board with the head away from you and cut down one side of the backbone. Insert the knife between flesh and bone and cut the fillet away with a slight sawing motion. Repeat with the second fillet. Turn the fish over and repeat as above.

To skin a whole flat fish, start with the dark skin and cut across the skin below the head and above the tail. Hold the tail firmly with kitchen paper and pull the skin from the head away in one whole piece. Turn the fish over and repeat with the white skin, if wished.

To skin fish fillets, place the fillet skin side down on a board and insert a sharp knife between flesh and skin. Work the knife along the length of the fillet with a slight sawing motion to free the flesh from the skin.

To prepare mussels and clams, discard any open shells and rinse the mussels or clams in running cold water for several minutes. Place them in a large bowl, cover with cold water and sprinkle over some brown flour or oatmeal. Leave to soak in a cool place for several hours. Wash again under running water and scrub the shells. Pull away the beard that often hangs down from the closed shell. Rinse again in several changes of cold water before cooking.

To clean squid, pull the head and tentacles away from the body, bringing the gut out of the body cavity. Reserve the tentacles, but discard the head and sharp 'beak'. Skin the squid by pulling it away from the body. Discard the 'wings' if wished. Wash the body cavity inside and out.

To shell and de-vein prawns, cut off the head and pull away the legs. Ease away and peel off the shell from the underneath of the prawn. Reserve the heads and shells; they make good stock. Using a sharp knife cut along the centre of the back and pull out and discard the black intestinal vein.

*Cooking fish and shellfish*
Poaching, stewing and steaming tend to keep a fish more moist than baking, grilling or barbecuing.

STEWING Fish can be stewed either whole or in pieces, cooked in flavoured stocks or sauces, where both fish and liquid are eaten as part of the dish. Stews are often made using a selection of vegetables, herbs, spices and stock.

STEAMING Whole fish, fillets or steaks are steamed in either a double boiler, or a fish kettle, over stock, where the delicate flavours can be enjoyed at their best. Often fish is cooked over a highly flavoured broth of marinade to impart flavour.

GRILLING Fish can be grilled under an oven grill, or over charcoal, which adds an intense flavour to the dish. Baste the fish with oil, butter or marinade as it cooks to prevent it becoming dry.

BAKING Fish can be open roasted in the oven, or cooked in a covered casserole or in a paper envelope (en papillote). Once in the oven you can forget about it until ready to serve, making this an ideal cooking method for a dinner party.

PAN FRYING This method is most commonly used to cook fillets, steaks or pieces of fish. Use a heavy non-stick frying pan and shallow fry the fish in oil or butter.

DEEP FRYING Use a deep, heavy-based pan, good-quality cooking oil and a sugar thermometer to successfully deep fry fish, which can be coated either in batter or in a little flour. The oil should reach approximately 180°C/360°F before you add the fish.

POACHING Cooking fish in a barely simmering liquid keeps it moist and tender. The liquid varies, but is generally plain water or court bouillon. Fish stock is often used if the stock is to be used as the basis of a sauce. Milk is usually used to poach smoked fish, as it helps to draw out excess saltiness. Beer and cider can also be used for poaching.

## COURT BOUILLON

≈

| | |
|---|---|
| 600 ml / 1 pint water | 2 celery sticks, sliced |
| 600 ml / 1 pint dry | 1 garlic clove |
| white wine | 2 bay leaves |
| 3 tbsp white wine vinegar | 2 sprigs fresh parsley |
| 2 carrots, sliced | 2 sprigs fresh thyme |
| 1 onion, chopped | 6 white peppercorns |
| 1 leek, sliced | 1 tsp salt |

≈

Place all the ingredients in a saucepan, bring slowly to the boil, cover and simmer for 30 minutes. Strain, and return to the pan. Boil rapidly for about 10 minutes until reduced to 600 ml/1 pint. Refrigerate until required.

## FISH STOCK

≈

Prepare as for Court Bouillon, increasing the water and wine to 900 ml/1½ pints, and adding 900 g/ 2 lb fish heads and trimmings. Boil until reduced to 900 ml/1½ pints.

# SOUPS AND STEWS

**F**ISH AND SEAFOOD *combined with a stock provide a delicious range of satisfying soups, broths and stews. The basis for many of these recipes, especially for those dishes that have a delicate flavour, is a good-quality fish stock (see page 7). Other dishes that contain more robust ingredients, imparting a richer and more intense flavour, can be made with vegetable stock. Make fish stock in large quantities and freeze the excess for future use. Ask your fishmonger to set aside some fish heads and bones to make the stock – these are usually available free of charge. I have included soups and stews from around the world, many of which are my versions of classic recipes. These range from quick and easy supper dishes, such as* Italian Fish Broth with Broccoli and Pasta, *to more elaborate stews, which are ideal for entertaining, such as* Exotic Seafood Stew *and* Tuna Fish Stew with Couscous.

# CONTENTS

≈

# EXOTIC SEAFOOD STEW

*Serves 4*

Based on a classic Spanish dish, this rich medley
of seafood is a visual feast. Although the
cooking time is quick, it is important to have all
the ingredients ready before you begin cooking,
to ensure success.

2 small cooked lobsters
(450 g/1 lb each)
4 tbsp olive oil
2 onions, chopped
2 garlic cloves, chopped
4 beef tomatoes, peeled
and chopped
¼ tsp powdered saffron
or turmeric
2 tbsp chopped fresh parsley
1 dried red chilli, seeded
and chopped
450 g/1 lb monkfish
fillet, cubed
Seasoned flour
6 fresh langoustines (Dublin
Bay prawns)
6 raw Mediterranean
(king) prawns

4 small squid (575 g/1¼ lb),
cleaned (see page 6) and cut
into rings
18 fresh mussels, scrubbed
18 fresh small clams, washed
4 tbsp brandy
75 ml/3 fl oz dry white wine
150 ml/¼ pint Fish Stock
(see page 7)
1 tsp salt
SAUCE
2 slices stale white bread,
crumbled
1 tbsp red wine vinegar
1 tbsp olive oil
25 g/1 oz cashew nuts, toasted
Pepper
Chopped fresh parsley, to
garnish

Prepare the lobsters: separate the head and body, and
break off the 2 claws from each lobster. Set aside.

Heat 1 tablespoon of the oil in a frying pan, and fry the
onion and garlic for 5 minutes. Add the tomatoes, saffron,
parsley and chilli, and fry for a further 10 minutes.
Transfer to a large flameproof casserole.

Dust the monkfish in a little seasoned flour. Heat the
remaining oil in the frying pan, add the monkfish, langoustines, prawns and squid, in that order, and fry until
browned. Add to the casserole with the mussels, clams
and prepared lobster.

Pour the brandy into the frying pan, ignite and flame.
When the flames die down pour any juices into the casserole with the wine, stock and salt. Bring to the boil, then
cover and simmer for 10 minutes.

Meanwhile, prepare the sauce. Soak the bread in the
vinegar and oil for 10 minutes. Add the nuts, and 6 tbsp
of the cooking juices from the casserole, and purée in a
blender until smooth. Stir back into the casserole until
combined, and simmer for a further 3-4 minutes, until the
sauce is thickened.

Adjust the seasoning, garnish with the chopped parsley,
and serve at once straight from the dish, with plenty of
bread to mop up the juices.

# TUNISIAN MUSSEL SOUP

*Serves 4*

A rich Tunisian soup of both puréed
and whole mussels is topped with a tangy lemon
and chilli garnish.

| | |
|---|---|
| 900 g/2 lb fresh small mussels, scrubbed | 400 g/14 oz can plum tomatoes, mashed |
| Pinch of saffron strands | 2 tbsp chopped fresh coriander |
| 1 tbsp olive oil | Salt and pepper |
| 1 onion, chopped | GARNISH |
| 2 garlic cloves, chopped | 4 tbsp olive oil |
| Grated rind and juice of 1 lemon | 1 shallot, thinly sliced |
| | Grated rind and juice of ½ lemon |
| 1 tsp paprika | |
| 1 tsp ground cumin | ½ small dried red chilli, seeded and sliced |
| Pinch of cayenne pepper | 1 tsp fresh thyme leaves |

Place the mussels in a large pan with just the water left on
the shells after scrubbing. Steam for 5-6 minutes until the
shells have opened. Discard any that remain closed.

Strain the cooking liquid into a bowl and make up to
600 ml/1 pint with water. Add the saffron strands and
leave to soak. Remove the mussels from their shells.

Heat the oil in a large pan, and fry the onion, garlic,
lemon rind and spices for 5 minutes. Add the tomatoes,
reserved saffron stock, half the cooked mussels, and the
lemon juice. Bring to the boil, cover and simmer for 20
minutes.

Purée the soup in a blender until very smooth, then
return to the pan. Add the remaining mussels, the coriander and seasoning, heat through, and keep warm.

For the garnish, heat the oil, and fry the shallot for 5
minutes until golden. Add the lemon rind and chilli, fry
for 3 minutes, stir in the lemon juice and thyme, and
remove from the heat. Serve the soup in individual bowls,
and spoon over the garnish.

# NORTH AFRICAN FISH STEW

*Serves 6*

This is an unusual tasting, but quite delicious
stew using a selection of fish and fish fillets.
The addition of dates and peanuts gives an
authentic North African flavour.

| | |
|---|---|
| 1 large aubergine, chopped | 1 small grey mullet, scaled, cleaned and cut into steaks |
| 4 tbsp groundnut oil | |
| 175 g/6 oz button mushrooms | 225 g/8 oz firm white fish fillets |
| 1 large onion, chopped | |
| 1 garlic clove, chopped | Juice of 3 limes |
| 2 green chillies, seeded and chopped | 150 ml/¼ pint vegetable stock |
| | 75 g/3 oz fresh dates, stoned and chopped |
| 1 tsp paprika | |
| 1 tsp ground cumin | 50 g/2 oz peanuts, toasted and roughly ground |
| 450 g/1 lb ripe tomatoes, chopped | Salt and pepper |
| 1 large mackerel, cleaned and cut into 2.5 cm/1 in steaks | |

Preheat the oven to 200°C/400°F/gas mark 6. Place the
aubergine in a roasting pan and toss with half the oil.
Bake on the top shelf of the oven for 20 minutes until
browned and tender.

Heat the remaining oil in a large pan, and stir-fry the
mushrooms for 3 minutes. Remove with a slotted spoon,
and set aside. Add the onion, garlic, chilli and spices to
the pan, and fry for 5 minutes. Add the aubergines, mushrooms, tomatoes, fish, lime juice and stock. Bring to the
boil, cover and simmer for 20 minutes.

Add the dates and peanuts to the stew, and simmer for a
further 5 minutes until the fish is cooked through.

Season to taste, and serve at once with boiled rice or
plenty of bread to soak up the juices.

*Top:* NORTH AFRICAN FISH STEW
*Bottom:* TUNISIAN MUSSEL SOUP

# SICILIAN SALT COD

*Serves 4-6*

Dried, salted cod must be soaked in plenty of cold water in order to soften the flesh and remove excess saltiness. I first tasted salt cod in Sicily cooked in a similar way to this recipe.

| | |
|---|---|
| 900 g/2 lb salt cod | 50 g/2 oz pitted black olives, |
| Milk | halved |
| 4 tbsp seasoned flour | 2 tbsp balsamic vinegar |
| 4 tbsp olive oil | 150 ml/¼ pint chicken or |
| 225 g/8 oz baby onions, | vegetable stock |
| halved | 2 tbsp tomato purée |
| 2 garlic cloves, chopped | 1 tsp sugar |
| 4 ripe tomatoes, chopped | Pepper |
| 100 g/4 oz sultanas | 2 tbsp chopped fresh parsley |

Wash the salt cod, place in a bowl, and cover with cold water. Leave to soak for 12 hours, changing the water several times, if possible.

Drain the fish, rinse under cold running water, and pat dry. Remove the skin, and cube the flesh. Place in a shallow dish, cover with milk, and leave to soak for a further 2 hours. Wash the fish again, pat dry, and dust lightly in the seasoned flour.

Heat half the oil in a non-stick frying pan, add the cod, and cook for 3 minutes until browned. Remove with a slotted spoon, and set aside.

Add the remaining oil to the pan, and fry the onions and garlic for 5 minutes until golden. Add the remaining ingredients except the parsley, bring to the boil, cover and simmer for 20 minutes.

Return the cod to the pan, sprinkle over the parsley, and simmer for a further 10-15 minutes until the fish is cooked. Season, and serve with rice, pasta or bread.

# TUNA FISH STEW WITH COUSCOUS

*Serves 4-6*

Couscous is usually served with a meat or vegetable stew, but here tuna, a very meaty fish, is used to make a tasty alternative.

| | |
|---|---|
| 350 g/12 oz couscous | 450 g/1 lb mixed vegetables |
| 600 ml/1 pint cold water | (e.g. carrots, fennel, celery, |
| 675 g/1½ lb fresh tuna steak | parsnip), sliced |
| 4 tbsp olive oil | 450 ml/¾ pint tomato juice |
| 1 red onion, cut into wedges | 250 ml/8 fl oz vegetable stock |
| 2 garlic cloves, chopped | 175 g/6 oz cooked chickpeas |
| 2 tsp ground coriander | 75 g/3 oz sultanas |
| 1 tsp ground cumin | 2 tbsp chopped fresh coriander |
| 1 tsp ground cinnamon | 25 g/1 oz pine nuts, toasted |
| ¼ tsp cayenne pepper | Fresh coriander sprigs, to garnish |

Place the couscous in a bowl, pour over the water, and set aside for 30 minutes for the grains to soften.

Cut the tuna into 2.5 cm/1 in cubes. Heat half the oil in a large pan, and quickly brown the tuna on all sides. Remove with a slotted spoon, and set aside.

Add the remaining oil to the pan, and fry the onion, garlic and spices for 5 minutes, then add the vegetables, and fry for a further 5 minutes. Stir in the tomato juice and stock, bring to the boil, cover and simmer for 20 minutes. Add the tuna, chickpeas, sultanas and coriander to the pan, and cook for a further 15 minutes.

Meanwhile, cook the couscous according to the instructions on the packet. Spoon the couscous onto a large platter. Using a slotted spoon, arrange the fish and vegetables over the couscous. Sprinkle over the nuts, garnish with coriander, and serve the juices separately.

*Top:* TUNA FISH STEW WITH COUSCOUS
*Bottom:* SICILIAN SALT COD

# STEWED SQUID WITH GARLIC CROSTINI

*Serves 4*

Based on a favourite dish I frequently enjoy at a local Italian restaurant, this squid stew makes a wonderful starter.

≈≈≈

900 g/2 lb squid, cleaned (see pages 6-7)
2 tbsp olive oil
1 onion, sliced
3 celery sticks, sliced
1 garlic clove, crushed
1 tbsp chopped fresh thyme
150 ml/¼ pint red wine
2 tbsp red wine vinegar
3 beef tomatoes, peeled, seeded and chopped

2 tbsp tomato purée
50 g/2 oz pitted black olives, halved
4 thick slices day old bread
2 garlic cloves, halved
salt and pepper
GARNISH
Lemon wedges
Flat-leafed parsley

≈≈≈

Cut the squid into 1 cm/½ in thick slices. Heat the oil in a pan, and quickly fry the squid until browned. Add the onion, celery, garlic and thyme, and fry for 10 minutes.

Add the wine, boil rapidly for 3 minutes then add the vinegar, tomatoes and tomato purée. Cover and simmer for 45 minutes, until the squid is really tender. Stir in the olives.

Preheat the oven to 200°C/400°F/gas mark 6. Prepare the crostini: place the sliced bread on a baking sheet, and bake for 15 minutes until crisp, turning once. Allow to cool slightly, and rub all over with the garlic halves.

Sit a slice of bread in each serving bowl, spoon over the squid and broth, and serve immediately, garnished with lemon wedges and flat-leafed parsley.

# FISH BROTH WITH BROCCOLI AND PASTA

*Serves 4*

This Italian soup is more of a stew than a soup and is a meal in itself. Serve with Italian-style bread and pass around some freshly grated Parmesan cheese.

≈≈≈

½ small onion, very finely chopped
1 garlic clove, crushed
25 g/1 oz sun-dried tomatoes in oil, drained and chopped
15 g/½ oz anchovies in oil, drained and chopped
1 tbsp chopped fresh parsley
¼ teaspoon freshly ground black pepper

1 tbsp olive oil
900 ml/1½ pints Fish Stock (see pages 6-7)
175 g/6 oz broccoli florets
100 g/4 oz conchiglie pasta shapes
Freshly grated Parmesan cheese, to serve

≈≈≈

Place the onion, garlic, tomatoes, anchovies, parsley, and pepper in a blender, and purée to form a fairly smooth paste.

Heat the oil in a large pan, add the paste, and fry gently for 5 minutes. Add the stock and bring to the boil. Stir in the broccoli and pasta, return to the boil, and simmer for 8-10 minutes, until the broccoli is cooked and the pasta is al dente.

Season to taste, and serve hot with freshly grated Parmesan and bread.

*Top:* FISH BROTH WITH BROCCOLI AND PASTA
*Bottom:* STEWED SQUID WITH GARLIC CROSTINI

# SOUPE AUX POISSONS

*Serves 4*

This is my version of the classic French dish, a creamy puréed soup full of the intense flavours of the sea.

≈

225 g/8 oz cooked prawns in shells
25 g/1 oz butter
1 onion, chopped
2 garlic cloves, chopped
2 ripe tomatoes, chopped
2 sprigs fresh parsley
2 sprigs fresh thyme
225 g/8 oz cod or haddock steaks
150 ml/¼ pint dry cider or dry white wine

900 ml/1½ pints vegetable stock
1 tbsp Worcestershire sauce or few drops of tabasco sauce
50 g/2 oz walnuts, toasted and ground
2 tbsp tomato purée
**TO SERVE**
½ quantity Garlic Sauce (see page 32), optional
Croûtons
Freshly grated Parmesan cheese

≈

Peel the prawns, and reserve the heads, shells and flesh.

Melt the butter in a large pan, and fry the onion and garlic for 3 minutes. Add the prawn shells and heads, tomatoes, herbs and fish, and fry for a further 3 minutes.

Pour in the cider or wine, boil rapidly for 3 minutes, then add the stock and Worcestershire sauce or tabasco. Cover and simmer for 30 minutes.

Purée the soup in a blender until smooth, and pass through a fine sieve into a clean pan.

Place the prawns in a blender with the walnuts, tomato purée and 2 tbsp of the puréed fish soup, and blend to form a thick paste. Whisk the paste back into the soup, and simmer for 5 minutes until thickened.

Spoon the soup into warmed serving bowls, stir in a spoonful of the garlic sauce (if using), and top with croûtons and Parmesan.

# FISH STEWED IN RED WINE

*Serves 4*

The addition of red wine gives a wonderful depth of flavour to this delightful stew. Discard the heads and tails of the fish if wished.

≈

4 small red snapper or silver bream (about 225 g/8 oz each), scaled and cleaned
2 tbsp plain flour
4 tbsp olive oil
225 g/8 oz button mushrooms
1 onion, sliced
1 garlic clove, chopped
1 red pepper, seeded and chopped
2 potatoes, diced

1 tbsp fennel seeds
450 g/1 lb ripe tomatoes, chopped (or 400 g/14 oz can chopped tomatoes)
600 ml/1 pint red wine
2 bay leaves
4 sprigs fresh thyme
Salt and pepper
Chopped fresh thyme, to garnish

≈

Wash and dry the fish, and dust lightly with the flour.

Heat the oil in a large wide pan, and fry the fish on both sides for 2-3 minutes until golden. Remove with a slotted spoon and set aside. Add the mushrooms to the pan, and fry for 3 minutes until golden. Remove with a slotted spoon and set aside.

Add a little extra oil to the pan if necessary, and fry the onion, garlic, pepper, potatoes and fennel seeds for 10 minutes. Add the tomatoes, wine, bay leaves and thyme, bring to the boil, and boil rapidly for 5 minutes until reduced. Cover and simmer gently for 10 minutes.

Return the fish and mushrooms to the pan, cover and simmer for a further 20 minutes until the fish is cooked.

Sprinkle over the chopped thyme, and serve with mashed potatoes or bread to soak up the juices.

*Top:* SOUPE AUX POISSONS
*Bottom:* FISH STEWED IN RED WINE

# SMOKED FISH CHOWDER

*Serves 6*

A recent trip to Seattle introduced me to the ingenious method of serving fish chowder in hollowed-out bread rolls. You will need to use large crusty rolls, served in soup bowls.

| | |
|---|---|
| 6 large crisp bread rolls | 600 ml/1 pint milk |
| 25 g/1 oz butter | 1 large potato, diced |
| 100 g/4 oz smoked bacon, diced | 225 g/8 oz un-dyed smoked haddock or cod, skinned |
| 1 onion, chopped | 150 ml/¼ pint single cream (optional) |
| 1 celery stick, sliced | 2 tbsp chopped fresh chives |
| 1 small red pepper, seeded and diced | Pinch of cayenne pepper |
| 300 ml/½ pint vegetable stock | Salt and pepper |

Preheat the oven to 200°C/400°F/gas mark 6. Cut the tops from each roll, scoop out and discard the middle, leaving the outer crust intact to act as a bowl. Bake in the oven for 8-10 minutes until crisp, place each roll in a soup bowl, and set aside.

Melt the butter in a large pan, and fry the bacon for 4-5 minutes until browned. Add the onion, celery and pepper, and fry for 5 minutes. Add the stock, milk and potatoes. Bring to the boil, cover and simmer for 10 minutes.

Cut the fish into bite-size pieces, add to the pan, and simmer for a further 10 minutes until the fish and potatoes are cooked.

Stir in the cream (if using), the chives and cayenne, and heat through for 1 minute. Adjust the seasoning, and spoon the chowder into the rolls.

# CRAB BISQUE

*Serves 4 - 6*

A delicious creamy puréed soup of fresh crab meat and butternut squash with a subtle hint of fresh ginger.

| | |
|---|---|
| 25 g/1 oz butter | 350 g/12 oz fresh crab meat |
| 1 onion, chopped | 900 ml/1½ pints vegetable or chicken stock |
| 2 celery sticks, chopped | |
| 2 tsp grated root ginger | Cayenne pepper |
| 450 g/1 lb butternut squash, chopped | Salt and pepper |
| | **GARNISH** |
| 150 ml/¼ pint dry white wine | Croûtons |
| | Freshly grated Parmesan cheese |

Melt the butter in a large pan, and fry the onion, celery and ginger for 5 minutes. Add the squash, and fry for a further 5 minutes.

Pour in the wine, and boil rapidly for 3 minutes, then stir in the crab meat, stock and cayenne pepper, bring to the boil, cover and simmer for 20 minutes.

Transfer the soup to a blender and purée until smooth. Return to the pan, reheat for 2 minutes, and season to taste. Serve the soup hot, garnished with the reserved crab meat, croûtons and freshly grated Parmesan.

*Top:* SMOKED FISH CHOWDER
*Bottom:* CRAB BISQUE

# HOT AND SOUR THAI FISH SOUP

*Serves 6*

One of the most famous of all Thai soups, with an exquisite combination of sweet, sour and hot.

~~~

| | |
|---|---|
| 450 g / 1 lb raw prawns in shells | 2 small green chillies, seeded and chopped |
| 1 onion, sliced | 4 coriander roots, washed and finely chopped (see page 80) |
| 2 slices fresh root ginger | 18 fresh small mussels, scrubbed |
| 2 stalks lemon grass, crushed | |
| 2 kaffir lime leaves, sliced or 1 tbsp grated lime rind | 2 tbsp light soy sauce |
| 1.2 litres / 2 pints vegetable stock | 6 small squid, cleaned (see pages 6-7) and cut into rings |
| 1 tbsp sunflower oil | 1 carrot, cut into matchsticks |
| 1 tsp sesame oil | 50 g / 2 oz watercress |
| 2 garlic cloves, crushed | |

~~~

Prepare the stock: peel the prawns, reserve the flesh, and place the shells and heads in a large pan. Add the onion, ginger, lemon grass, lime leaves or rind and the stock. Bring to the boil, cover and simmer for 30 minutes. Strain into a clean pan.

Heat the sunflower oil and sesame oil in a small pan. Add the garlic, chillies and coriander root, and fry for 3 minutes until softened. Purée in a blender to form a smooth paste, and set aside.

Place the mussels in a pan with just the water left on the shells after scrubbing. Steam for 4-5 minutes until the shells have opened. Discard any that remain closed. Strain the liquid through a fine sieve into a bowl, whisk in the garlic paste, and stir into the strained lemon grass stock. Allow the mussels to cool slightly, remove from their shells and set aside.

Add the prawns and squid to the stock, simmer for 5 minutes, then add the carrots. Simmer for 3 minutes, and finally add the cooked mussels and watercress leaves. Heat through for a further minute, and serve at once.

# COCONUT FISH SOUP

*Serves 6*

The classic Thai ingredients of lemon grass, lime leaves, ginger and coconut lend a truly authentic flavour to this rich fish soup.

~~~

| | |
|---|---|
| 2 stalks lemon grass, halved and lightly crushed | 1 tsp ground turmeric |
| 4 slices fresh root ginger | 400 g / 14 oz can coconut milk |
| 4 kaffir lime leaves, shredded or 1 tbsp grated lime rind | 550 g / 1¼ lb mixed fish fillets (e.g. cod, monkfish, plaice and hake) |
| 2 tbsp chopped fresh coriander | |
| 900 ml / 1½ pints vegetable stock or water | 2 tbsp light soy sauce |
| | GARNISH |
| 1 tbsp sunflower oil | Sesame oil |
| 1 onion, finely chopped | Lime juice |
| 1 green chilli, seeded and chopped | Fresh coriander leaves |

~~~

Place the lemon grass, ginger, lime leaves or grated rind and coriander in a pan. Add half the stock or water, bring to the boil, cover and simmer gently for 30 minutes. Remove from the heat, and set aside.

Heat the oil in a large pan and fry the onion, chilli and turmeric for 5 minutes. Add the coconut milk, remaining stock, fish fillets and soy sauce, and bring to the boil. Lower the heat, and simmer very gently for 5-8 minutes until the fish is tender. Using a slotted spoon, transfer the fish to warmed soup bowls.

Strain the lemon grass stock into the coconut stock, bring to the boil, and simmer for 5 minutes.

Pour the stock over the fish, and serve at once, drizzled with a little sesame oil and lime juice, and garnished with coriander leaves.

*Top:* HOT AND SOUR THAI FISH SOUP
*Bottom:* COCONUT FISH SOUP

# TOMATO SOUP WITH FISH QUENELLES

*Serves 6*

Quenelles are made from a mousse-like mixture of puréed fish, cream and egg whites, which is then shaped into ovals and lightly poached. It is important to keep the mixture as cool as possible to achieve a light fluffy texture.

| | |
|---|---|
| 2 tbsp olive oil | 300 ml/½ pint chicken or |
| 1 onion, chopped | vegetable stock |
| 2 garlic cloves, crushed | 2 tbsp chopped fresh basil |
| 900 g/2 lb ripe tomatoes, | fresh basil leaves, to garnish |
| chopped | **QUENELLES** |
| 1 tbsp chopped fresh parsley | 225 g/8 oz smoked cod fillet |
| 2 tsp chopped fresh thyme | Grated rind of ½ lemon |
| 150 ml/¼ pint dry | Salt and pepper |
| white wine | 2 small egg whites (size 5) |
| | 75 ml/3 fl oz single cream |

Prepare the quenelles: skin and remove any bones from the cod, and purée in a blender with the lemon rind and plenty of seasoning until very smooth. Blend in the egg whites, and transfer to a bowl. Half fill a larger bowl with ice, and sit the bowl of fish purée on top. Gradually beat in the cream, a little at a time. Chill for 2 hours.

To make the soup: heat the oil in a pan, and fry the onion and garlic for 5 minutes. Add the tomatoes, parsley, thyme and wine, and boil rapidly for 5 minutes. Add the stock, cover and simmer for 30 minutes. Purée the soup, pass through a sieve into a pan, and stir in the basil.

To cook the quenelles: bring a large pan of water to a steady simmer. Form the chilled fish purée into ovals by passing the mixture from one spoon to another to make egg-shaped mousses. Poach the quennelles in the gently simmering water for about 1 minute, or until they rise to the surface. Drain on paper towels.

Quickly reheat the soup, and serve each portion topped with 3 quenelles, garnished with basil leaves.

# MUSSEL AND SCALLOP SOUP WITH CHIVES

*Serves 4*

A lovely soup perfect for special guests at a dinner party. The more flavour you get from the fish stock, the more delicious the end result will be.

| | |
|---|---|
| 12 fresh scallops, cleaned | 150 ml/¼ pint dry white |
| 25 g/1 oz unsalted butter | wine |
| 2 small leeks, shredded | 6 white peppercorns |
| 20 fresh mussels, scrubbed | 600 ml/1 pint Fish Stock |
| 1 onion, chopped | (see pages 6-7) |
| 2 sprigs parsley | 150 ml/¼ pint single cream |
| | 2 tbsp chopped fresh chives |

Separate the scallops from their corals, cut the white flesh in half, and set aside.

Melt half the butter in a small pan, and fry the leeks for 2 minutes until softened. Transfer to serving bowls, and keep warm while preparing the soup.

Put the mussels, onion, parsley, wine and peppercorns in a large pan, and steam for 4–5 minutes until all the mussel shells are opened. Discard any that remain closed. Allow to cool slightly, then carefully remove the mussels from their shells, and set aside.

Strain the cooking liquid through a fine sieve into a clean pan, add the fish stock, bring to the boil, and simmer until reduced by half.

Add the scallops to the stock, and simmer for 2 minutes, then add the cooked mussels, and heat through. Using a slotted spoon, transfer the shellfish to the soup bowls, and arrange on top of the leeks.

Stir the cream and chives into the stock, and boil rapidly until reduced slightly. Season to taste, and pour into the bowls. Serve immediately.

*Top Right:* TOMATO SOUP WITH FISH QUENELLES
*Bottom Left:* MUSSEL AND SCALLOP SOUP WITH CHIVES

# APPETIZERS
# AND STARTERS

THIS SECOND CHAPTER *is full of exciting ideas to serve as pre-dinner nibbles to stimulate the appetite, delicious starters for a dinner party, or even a light lunch or snack meal. Tapenade and Anchoiade spread on crispy garlic bread and topped with grilled peppers, tomatoes and cheese make a stunning plate of tasty hors d'oeuvres. This particular dish is one of my favourites and is always popular with my guests.*

*I find starters are often the most tempting dishes, so I have tried to include a varied selection, inspired by cuisines from all around the world. They include many classics that I have enjoyed on travels and have adapted for this book, including the* Stuffed Filo Prawn Fingers, *a Goan speciality, and the equally delicious Italian antipasti,* Fresh Tuna and Bean Salad.

# CONTENTS

≋

# GRILLED HERRING TOASTS

*Serves 6*

A quick and easy toasted sandwich, this makes a perfect brunch or light lunch.

≈

| | |
|---|---|
| 6 medium herrings, filleted | Lemon juice |
| 6 large slices of bread | Salt and pepper |
| 1 tbsp wholegrain mustard | Soured cream or yogurt, to |
| 50 g/2 oz butter | serve |
| 1 tbsp chopped fresh tarragon | |

≈

Preheat the grill. Cut the herring fillets through the back, and using a small pair of tweezers, pull out any larger bones. Lightly grill the bread on both sides.

Cream the mustard, butter and tarragon together, and spread a little over 1 side of the toasted bread. Place 2 halved herring fillets on each slice, trimming the fillets to the size of the bread. Spread over the remaining mustard butter.

Squeeze a little lemon juice over each one, season, and return to the grill for 5-6 minutes until the fish is cooked through.

Serve at once with soured cream or yogurt, if wished.

# SMOKED MACKEREL AND ORANGE PATE

*Serves 4*

As you bite into this tangy pâté the delicious green peppercorns explode in the mouth, adding both texture and a fiery flavour.

≈

| | |
|---|---|
| 225 g/8 oz smoked mackerel fillet, skinned and boned | Squeeze of lemon juice |
| 25 g/1 oz butter, softened | 150 ml/¼ pint low-fat cream cheese |
| 2 tbsp freshly squeezed orange juice | 1 tbsp green peppercorns, |
| 2 tbsp cointreau or orange juice | Lightly crushed Melba toast, French bread or vegetable |
| 2 tbsp chopped fresh chives | crudités, to serve |

≈

Place the mackerel in a bowl, and mash well with a fork. Beat in the remaining ingredients to form a fairly coarse paste. Transfer to a bowl, cover and chill for 1 hour.

Remove the pâté from the refrigerator at least 30 minutes before serving to return to room temperature. Serve with melba toast, French bread or a selection of vegetable crudités.

*Top:* GRILLED HERRING TOASTS
*Bottom:* SMOKED MACKEREL AND ORANGE PATE

# WARM SMOKED FISH MOUSSE

*Serves 4*

The flavour of smoked fish, combined with a light texture, makes these mousses a perfect dinner party starter.

| | |
|---|---|
| 450 g/1 lb un-dyed smoked fish, skinned and boned | **TOMATO VINAIGRETTE** |
| Grated rind of ½ lemon | 2 tbsp olive oil |
| 1 tbsp cognac | 4 ripe tomatoes, peeled, seeded and diced |
| 3 egg whites | 2 shallots, finely chopped |
| 2 tbsp chopped fresh tarragon | 1 tbsp shredded fresh basil |
| 2 tsp hot horseradish sauce | Juice of ½ lemon |
| White pepper | Salt and pepper |
| 150 ml/¼ pint single cream | Fresh herbs, to garnish |

Cube the smoked fish, place in a blender with the lemon rind and cognac, and purée until very smooth. Transfer to a bowl, and gradually beat in the egg whites, tarragon, horseradish and pepper. Cover and chill for 2 hours.

Preheat the oven to 180°C/350°F/gas mark 4. Half fill a roasting pan with boiling water, and place on the middle shelf of the oven. Remove the fish purée from the refrigerator, and sit the bowl in a larger bowl filled with crushed ice. Gradually whisk in the cream until incorporated, and spoon into 4 greased ramekin dishes.

Place the ramekins in the roasting pan, and bake for 25-30 minutes until mousses are risen and firm to the touch. Remove from the oven, and leave to rest for 5 minutes.

Meanwhile, prepare the vinaigrette: heat the oil in a small pan, stir in the tomatoes, shallots and basil, and heat gently for 5 minutes. Remove from the heat and whisk in the lemon juice and seasonings. Keep warm.

Un-mould the mousses onto individual plates, pour over a little of the tomato vinaigrette, and serve at once, garnished with basil or tarragon sprigs.

# BAKED STUFFED TOMATOES

*Serves 6*

Tomatoes and crab combine well together. Here the tomatoes are stuffed with a mixture of crab meat and breadcrumbs, and baked until soft and golden.

| | |
|---|---|
| 6 beef tomatoes | 100 g/4 oz fresh white breadcrumbs |
| 3 tbsp olive oil | 2 tbsp chopped fresh parsley |
| 1 small onion, finely chopped | 1 tbsp wholegrain mustard |
| 1 garlic clove, crushed | 50 g/2 oz freshly grated Parmesan cheese |
| 225 g/8 oz fresh white crab meat | Salt and pepper |

Preheat the oven to 200°C/400°F/gas mark 6. Cut the tops from the tomatoes, and carefully scoop out the flesh. Chop finely and reserve.

Heat the oil in a frying pan, and fry the onion and garlic for 5 minutes until browned. Stir in the chopped tomato, crab meat, breadcrumbs, parsley, mustard, and two-thirds of the cheese. Season to taste.

Spoon the filling into the hollowed out tomato shells, piling the mixture up.

Transfer the tomatoes to a baking dish, sprinkle over the remaining cheese, drizzle with a little extra olive oil and bake for 40 minutes until softened and the filling brown. Serve at once with a crisp green salad.

*Top:* WARM SMOKED FISH MOUSSE
*Bottom:* BAKED STUFFED TOMATOES

# SALT COD FRITTERS WITH GARLIC SAUCE

*Serves 8-12*

These tasty salt cod fritters remind me of glorious sunny days in Greece. The fritters can be cooked ahead of time and crisped up in a hot oven, just before serving.

| | |
|---|---|
| 900 g/2 lb salt cod | 4 tbsp water |
| Milk | 2 garlic cloves, chopped |
| **BATTER** | 1 tbsp lemon juice |
| 100 g/4 oz plain flour | Pinch of cayenne pepper |
| 1 tsp salt | 6 tbsp olive oil |
| 200 ml/7 fl oz milk | Vegetable oil, for deep frying |
| 2 tbsp ouzo or brandy | 4 tbsp flour |
| 1 egg, lightly beaten | **GARNISH** |
| 2 tbsp chopped fresh coriander | Lemon wedges |
| **GARLIC SAUCE** | Fresh coriander sprigs |
| 2-3 slices of stale white bread, crusts removed | |

Prepare the salt cod (see page 14).

Make the batter: sift the flour and salt into a large bowl, and make a well in the centre. Gradually beat in the milk, ouzo or brandy and egg to form a smooth pouring batter. Stir in the coriander, and leave to rest for 30 minutes.

Meanwhile, make the garlic sauce: pour the water over the bread and soak for 5 minutes. Squeeze out the water, place the bread, garlic, lemon juice and cayenne in a blender, and purée to form a thick paste. Gradually work in the oil, a little at a time, to form a thick sauce, thinning with 2-3 tbsp boiling water if the sauce is too thick. Transfer to a bowl, cover and set aside.

To fry: heat the oil in a deep, heavy-based pan to 180°C/350°F or until a cube of bread browns in 30 seconds. Dust the cubes of salt cod with a little seasoned flour, dip in the batter, and deep fry in batches for 4-5 minutes until crisp and golden. Drain on kitchen paper.

Serve with the garlic sauce.

# CLARE'S STUFFED PEPPERS

*Serves 6*

Although this is a version of a classic Italian dish from Piedmont, I have named it after a friend who always cooks the peppers to perfection.

| | |
|---|---|
| 50 g/2 oz can anchovies in oil, drained | 3 large ripe tomatoes, peeled and quartered |
| Milk | Salt and pepper |
| 1 garlic clove, crushed | 6 tbsp olive oil |
| 1 tbsp chopped fresh basil | 1 tbsp balsamic vinegar |
| 3 peppers, red, yellow or orange | Fresh basil sprigs, to garnish |

Preheat the oven to 220°C/425°F/gas mark 7. Place the anchovy fillets in a small dish, cover with milk, and leave to soak for 10 minutes. Drain, wash well and pat dry. Chop finely, and mix with the garlic and basil.

Cut the peppers in half through the stalks. Scoop out the seeds, and arrange in a roasting pan, cut side up.

Place 2 tomato quarters in each pepper half, and divide the anchovy mixture between the peppers. Season well.

Whisk together the oil and vinegar, pour into the peppers, and bake for about 1 hour until golden and caramelized.

Serve hot, garnished with basil, or allow to cool to room temperature, and serve with a salad and crisp French bread to mop up the juices.

*Top:* SALT COD FRITTERS WITH GARLIC SAUCE
*Bottom:* CLARE'S STUFFED PEPPERS

# SOLE FILLETS WITH WARM CAPER DRESSING

*Serves 4*

All credit must go to my dear friend Judy Ridgway, who served a version of this wonderful dish to me at a memorable dinner party.

| | |
|---|---|
| *2 large lemon sole, skinned, filleted and cut in half lengthways* | *1 tbsp chopped fresh dill* |
| | *4 sun-dried tomatoes in oil, drained and sliced* |
| *4 tbsp dry white wine* | *Grated rind of ½ orange* |
| *2 tbsp orange juice* | *2 tsp balsamic or red wine vinegar* |
| *Salt and pepper* | |
| *6 tbsp olive oil* | *Lamb's lettuce, to garnish* |
| *4 tbsp drained capers, washed and dried* | |

Preheat the oven to 220°C/425°F/gas mark 7. Roll up each halved sole fillet, secure with cocktail sticks, and arrange in a baking dish in a single layer.

Add the wine and orange juice, season well, cover with foil, and bake for 20 minutes or until the sole is cooked through, feeling firm to the touch.

Meanwhile, heat half the oil in a small pan, and stir in the capers, dill, tomatoes and orange rind. Heat gently until almost boiling, remove from the heat and keep warm.

Strain the fish juices from the sole fillets into the pan with the capers. Cover the sole fillets with foil to keep warm. Bring the sauce to the boil, whisk in the remaining oil and the vinegar, and simmer for 1 minute.

Arrange 2 sole fillets on each plate, pour over the warm dressing, and serve at once, garnished with the salad leaves.

# CELERIAC ROSTIS WITH SMOKED SALMON

*Serves 4*

Celeriac is used here instead of the more traditional potato, to make mouth-watering rostis. Topped with smoked salmon and soured cream they make a delicious dinner party starter.

| | |
|---|---|
| *350 g/12 oz celeriac, peeled and grated* | *1 egg, lightly beaten* |
| | *Oil for shallow frying* |
| *½ small onion, very thinly sliced* | *225 g/8 oz smoked salmon* |
| *1 tbsp chopped fresh chives* | *4 tbsp soured cream or natural yogurt* |
| *½ tsp salt* | *Salt and pepper* |
| *1 tsp grated fresh horseradish* | *Chopped fresh chives, to garnish* |
| *15 g/½ oz self-raising flour* | |

Place the grated celeriac in a large bowl, and stir in the onion, chives, salt, horseradish and flour. Beat in the egg until evenly combined.

Heat about 1 cm/½ in oil in a non-stick frying pan. Divide the celeriac mixture into 8, spoon half into the hot oil, pressing each one flat to make a small pancake or rosti. Fry for 3-4 minutes on each side until crisp and golden. Drain on kitchen paper, and keep warm while cooking the remaining mixture.

Place 2 rostis on each plate. Top with the salmon and a spoonful of soured cream, and garnish with chopped chives.

*Top:* CELERIAC ROSTIS WITH SMOKED SALMON
*Bottom:* SOLE FILLETS WITH WARM CAPER DRESSING

# TAPENADE AND ANCHOIADE CROSTINI

*Serves 4 - 8*

These tangy spreads make delicious toppings for crostini or bruschetta. Both mixtures can be prepared ahead of time, and stored in a sealed jar in the refrigerator for several weeks.

**TAPENADE**
50 g/2 oz can anchovies in oil, drained
Milk
100 g/4 oz pitted black olives
2 tbsp drained capers, washed
1 garlic clove, crushed
1 tsp grated lemon rind
2 tbsp chopped fresh parsley
4 tbsp light olive oil
**ANCHOIADE**
2 x 50 g/2 oz cans anchovies in oil, drained
Milk
2 garlic cloves, crushed
2 tbsp chopped fresh basil
2 tsp lemon juice

25 g/1 oz almonds, toasted and ground
4 tbsp olive oil
Salt and pepper
**CROSTINI**
8 thick slices ciabatta or rustic French bread
2 garlic cloves
olive oil, to drizzle
**TOPPINGS**
Topping 1: grilled peppers, goat cheese and rocket leaves
Topping 2: sliced plum tomatoes, crushed garlic, basil leaves
Topping 3: grilled chicory halves
Topping 4: grilled fennel slices

For the tapenade: soak the anchovy fillets in milk for 10 minutes. Drain, wash well, and pat dry.

Roughly chop the anchovies, and combine with the remaining ingredients. Pound in a mortar or purée in a blender to form a fairly smooth paste. Cover and set aside.

For the anchoiade: prepare as for tapenade.

For the crostini: grill the bread lightly on both sides, rub all over with garlic, and then drizzle with olive oil.

Spread either the tapenade or anchoiade over one side of each slice. Top with any of the suggested toppings, return to the grill for a few seconds, and serve immediately.

# FRESH TUNA AND BEAN SALAD

*Serves 4*

The wonderful flavour and texture of fresh tuna is worth the extra expense, as it transforms this dish into a very memorable salad.

450 g/1 lb fresh tuna steak, cubed
4 tbsp olive oil
1 garlic clove, crushed
400 g/14 oz can flageolet or haricot beans, drained
1 red onion, thinly sliced

2 ripe plum tomatoes, peeled, seeded and diced
2 tbsp chopped fresh parsley
1 tbsp chopped fresh basil
2 tsp balsamic vinegar
Salt and pepper
100 g/4 oz rocket or salad leaves

Heat half the oil in a frying pan, add the tuna, cover and fry over a low heat for 4-5 minutes until cooked – it should still be a little pink in the centre.

Transfer the fish and all the pan juices to a large bowl, and stir in the garlic, beans, onion, tomatoes and herbs.

Blend the remaining oil with the vinegar and seasonings, pour over the salad, toss well, and leave to marinate for 1 hour.

Stir in the rocket leaves, and serve immediately.

*Top:* FRESH TUNA AND BEAN SALAD
*Bottom:* TAPENADE AND ANCHOIADE CROSTINI

# STUFFED FILO PRAWN FINGERS

*Serves 4*

I tasted a similar dish to these prawn fingers in Goa, where the prawns were wrapped in soft poppadoms and fried. I have substituted filo pastry with great success.

| | |
|---|---|
| 2 spring onions, finely chopped | 3 sheets filo pastry |
| 1 tbsp chopped fresh coriander | 2 tbsp olive oil |
| 1 garlic clove, crushed | 12 cooked Mediterranean |
| 1 tsp grated fresh root ginger | (king) prawns, shelled and |
| 1 small fresh red chilli, seeded | de-veined (see pages 6-7) |
| and chopped | Vegetable oil, for deep frying |
| 1 tsp tamarind paste or | Chilli Soy Dip, to serve |
| lemon juice | (optional) |
| 1 tbsp tomato purée | |

Place the spring onions, coriander, garlic, ginger, chilli, tamarind paste or lemon juice and tomato purée in a blender, and purée to form a smooth paste.

Cut each sheet of pastry lengthways into 4 strips 20 x 8 cm/8 x 3 in. Take one strip and brush with a little of the oil, spread ½ tsp of the chilli paste along one narrow end, and place a prawn over the top, with only the tail extending beyond the edge of the pastry. Roll up to enclose the prawn, twisting the ends together to seal. Cover with a clean tea towel and repeat to make 12 fingers.

Heat 10 cm/4 in oil in a heavy-based pan to a temperature of 180°C/350°F or until a cube of bread browns in 30 seconds. Carefully slip in the prawn fingers, and cook for 2 minutes until the pastry is crisp and golden.

Drain on absorbent paper, and serve at once with the chilli soy dip (see opposite).

# THAI PRAWN BALLS WITH CHILLI SOY DIP

*Serves 4 - 6*

These crispy Thai-style prawn balls are delicious dipped into the chilli soy sauce.

| | |
|---|---|
| 350 g/12 oz cooked peeled prawns | 2 tbsp flour |
| 50 g/2 oz fresh breadcrumbs | 1 egg, beaten |
| ½ small onion, very finely chopped | 50 g/2 oz desiccated coconut |
| 1 garlic clove, crushed | Vegetable oil, for deep frying |
| 1 tbsp chopped fresh coriander | DIP |
| Grated rind and juice of ½ lime | 1 small red chilli, seeded and sliced |
| 1 small green chilli, seeded and chopped | 1 tbsp lime juice |
| ¼ tsp five spice powder | 2 tbsp dark soy sauce |
| | 2 tbsp water |
| | 1 tbsp soft brown sugar |

Place the prawns, breadcrumbs, onion, garlic, coriander, lime juice and rind, chilli and spice in a blender, and purée to form a smooth paste. Chill for 30 minutes.

Divide the prawn mixture into 12 and roll each piece into small balls. Dust lightly with flour, and dip into the egg, and then the coconut, to completely coat the balls. Chill for a further 30 minutes.

Meanwhile, prepare the dip: place all the ingredients in a small pan, and heat gently to dissolve the sugar. Set aside to cool.

Heat the oil in a heavy-based pan, and fry the balls in batches for 3-4 minutes until crisp and golden. Drain on kitchen paper, and keep warm while frying the remaining balls. Serve hot with the dip.

*Top:* STUFFED FILO PRAWN FINGERS
*Bottom:* THAI PRAWN BALLS WITH CHILLI SOY DIP

## JAPANESE PRAWN TEMPURA

*Serves 6*

To ensure the batter for the prawns is light and crispy, make it at the last minute and do not over beat the mixture – it should be slightly lumpy. For the dipping sauce, use tamari, which is the slightly thicker type of soy sauce.

| | |
|---|---|
| *30 large raw prawns in shells* | *15 g/½ oz daikon, grated* |
| **DIPPING SAUCE** | *vegetable oil, for deep frying* |
| *2 tbsp tamari soy sauce* | **BATTER** |
| *2 tbsp lemon juice* | *1 large egg (size 1)* |
| *2 tbsp sake or sweet sherry* | *100 g/4 oz plain flour, sifted* |
| *1 tsp clear honey* | *150 ml/¼ pint cold water* |
| *1 spring onion, shredded* | |

Remove the head and shells from the prawns, and cut out the vein from the back of the prawn. Wash and pat dry. Combine the ingredients for the sauce, and set aside.

To make the batter: lightly beat the egg until the yolk is broken and starting to blend with the white. Stir in the flour and then the water, until just combined. Do not over mix the batter; there should still be a few lumps in the mixture. Set the batter bowl in a larger bowl filled with ice cubes.

Heat about 12 cm/4 in of oil in a deep heavy-based pan to a temperature of 180°C/350°F on a sugar thermometer, or until a cube of bread browns in 30 seconds.

Holding the prawns by the tails, dip into the batter, and then carefully slip them into the hot oil. Fry the prawns five at a time for about 2 minutes until the batter is golden and very crisp. Drain on kitchen paper, and keep warm while frying the remaining prawns.

Serve at once with the dipping sauce.

## SCALLOPS WITH BLACK BEAN SAUCE

*Serves 4*

Fermented black beans are available in cans from Oriental stores. Wash several times in cold water to extract the excess saltiness.

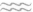

| | |
|---|---|
| *12 fresh scallops on the shell* | *2 tsp grated fresh root ginger* |
| *2 tbsp fermented black beans* | *4 tbsp light soy sauce* |
| *2 spring onions, thinly sliced* | *2 tbsp dry sherry* |
| *½ red pepper, seeded and* | *Juice of 1 lemon* |
| *thinly sliced* | |

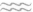

Carefully remove the scallops from the shells by snipping through the muscle that attaches them. Wash and reserve the shells. Wash the scallops, pat dry, and place in a shallow dish.

Wash the beans well, and add to the dish with the remaining ingredients except the lemon juice. Cover and marinate for at least 1 hour.

Transfer the scallops and their marinade to a heatproof plate and pour over the lemon juice. Set a trivet in a large pan with about 2.5 cm/1 in of water, and bring to the boil. Sit the plate on the trivet, cover the pan with a lid, and simmer gently for 3-4 minutes until the scallops are just tender.

Return the scallops to their shells with all the cooking liquid, and serve immediately.

*Top:* JAPANESE PRAWN TEMPURA
*Bottom:* SCALLOPS WITH BLACK BEAN SAUCE

# LANGOUSTINES WITH THREE DIPS

*Serves 4*

Serve as a starter, with one or all three dips as accompaniments. Use fresh large Mediterranean (king) prawns if you cannot find langoustines.

| | |
|---|---|
| 20-24 fresh langoustines (Dublin Bay prawns) | ½ tsp cumin seeds, toasted |
| Lemon wedges, to garnish | ½ tsp paprika |
| **PEPPER DIP** | Pinch of cayenne pepper |
| ½ red pepper, halved and seeded | 50 ml/2 fl oz olive oil |
| 1 small garlic clove, crushed | 1 tbsp balsamic vinegar |
| 2 tbsp olive oil | 2 tbsp boiling water |
| Yolk of 1 hard-boiled egg, chopped | **SESAME AND GINGER DIP** |
| 1 tbsp chopped fresh parsley | 50 ml/2 fl oz mayonnaise |
| **SPICED DIP** | 1 tsp sesame oil |
| 1 garlic clove, crushed | 1 tsp grated fresh root ginger |
| | 1 tsp orange juice |
| | Pinch of five spice powder |

Wash and dry the langoustines. Bring a large pan of water to a rolling boil, plunge in the langoustines, return to the boil, and poach for 3 minutes. Drain, refresh briefly under cold running water, and leave to go cold.

Meanwhile, prepare the dips. For the pepper dip, grill the pepper for 5 minutes on each side until charred and softened. Cool, peel, and discard the skin. Purée the flesh in a blender, then gradually blend in the remaining ingredients to form a smooth sauce. Cover and set aside.

For the spiced dip, place the crushed garlic and spices in a grinder, and blend to form a fairly smooth paste. Transfer to a bowl and very gradually whisk in the oil, then the vinegar, and finally the water, to form a thin pouring consistency. Cover and set aside.

For the sesame and ginger dip, combine all the ingredients in a bowl until evenly blended. Cover and set aside.

Serve the poached langoustines on a large platter with the 3 dips. Garnish and serve with fresh bread.

# SCALLOP AND PARMA HAM KEBABS

*Serves 4*

The salsa for the kebabs can be made in advance and kept in the refrigerator for several hours.

| | |
|---|---|
| 20 large fresh scallops | **SALSA** |
| 10 thin slices Parma ham | 1 ripe mango, peeled, stoned and diced |
| 20 large sage leaves | 2 ripe tomatoes, peeled, seeded and diced |
| Selection of salad leaves, to serve | 1 fresh green chilli, seeded and diced |
| **MARINADE** | 2 tbsp chopped fresh chervil |
| 2 tbsp chopped fresh chervil | ½ red onion, finely chopped |
| 1 tsp fennel seeds, toasted and crushed | Juice of 1 lime |
| 2 sprigs rosemary | 2 tbsp hazelnut oil |
| 150 ml/¼ pint dry white wine | ½ tsp sugar |
| 4 tbsp hazelnut oil | Salt and pepper |

Wash the scallops. Cut away the tough grey membrane from each one, and pat dry.

Cut each slice of Parma ham in half lengthways to form 20 long thin strips.

Wrap a sage leaf, and then a strip of ham around each scallop, to form small parcels. Thread onto 4 skewers and place in a shallow dish.

Combine the marinade ingredients, and pour over the kebabs. Cover and marinate for 2 hours.

Meanwhile, make the salsa: combine all the ingredients, season to taste, and set aside for the flavours to infuse.

Preheat the grill. Remove the scallop parcels from their marinade, brush with the marinade and grill for 2-3 minutes on each side until charred and firm to the touch.

Serve the kebabs at once, with a little salsa and a selection of salad leaves.

*Top:* SCALLOP AND PARMA HAM KEBABS
*Bottom:* LANGOUSTINES WITH THREE DIPS

## MARINATED HERRING SALAD

*Serves 4*

A typical Scandinavian recipe using raw herring which is marinated in lemon juice to "cook" the flesh and then served with a beetroot and apple salad.

| | |
|---|---|
| *450 g/1 lb very fresh herring, filleted* | *2 tbsp soured cream* |
| *Juice of 4 lemons* | *½ tsp creamed horseradish* |
| *100 g/4 oz cooked beetroot, diced* | *2 tsp chopped fresh tarragon* |
| *1 eating apple, cored and diced* | *Salt and pepper* |
| *75 g/3 oz cucumber, diced* | **GARNISH** |
| | *Radicchio leaves* |
| | *Sliced red onion* |

Wash and dry the herring fillets. Using a pair of fine tweezers, pull out any small bones. Place the fillets skin-side down in a large shallow dish, to fit in a single layer. Pour over the lemon juice, cover and refrigerate overnight. Allow the fish to return to room temperature for about 1 hour before serving.

Mix together the beetroot, apple, cucumber, soured cream, horseradish, tarragon, seasonings, and 1 tbsp of the herring marinade. Set aside to infuse for 1 hour.

Remove the herring fillets from the marinade, and cut into bite-size pieces.

Arrange the fillets on plates with a spoonful of the beetroot relish, and garnish with radicchio leaves and slices of red onion.

## CARPACCIO WITH AVOCADO SALSA

*Serves 6*

You will need a very sharp knife to cut the raw haddock into wafer thin slices so that it can "cook" in the citrus marinade.

| | |
|---|---|
| *675 g/1½ lb very fresh haddock fillet* | **AVOCADO SALSA** |
| *Grated rind of 1 lime* | *½ onion, finely chopped* |
| *Juice of 3 limes* | *2 ripe tomatoes, peeled, seeded and diced* |
| *1 fresh green chilli, seeded and sliced* | *1 ripe avocado, peeled, stoned and diced* |
| *4 spring onions, sliced* | *Juice of ½ lime* |
| *1 tsp coriander seeds, crushed* | *1 garlic clove, crushed* |
| *2 sprigs fresh thyme* | *Pinch of salt* |
| *4 sprigs fresh chervil* | *Pinch of sugar* |
| *6 tbsp olive oil* | *2 tbsp chopped fresh coriander* |
| | *1 tbsp olive oil* |

Wash and dry the haddock and pull out any remaining bones. Using a very sharp knife, cut the fish on an angle into paper thin slices, and place in a shallow dish.

Combine all the remaining ingredients, pour over the fish, and marinate for 1 hour at room temperature.

Meanwhile, prepare the salsa: mix all the ingredients together, cover and set aside.

Remove the haddock from its marinade, and arrange on plates with a spoonful of the salsa.

*Top:* MARINATED HERRING SALAD
*Bottom:* HADDOCK CARPACCIO WITH AVOCADO SALSA

# SIMPLE SUPPER DISHES

M OST OF US *today have busy schedules and hectic lifestyles so fish provides the* *perfect answer, as it generally cooks quickly. The recipes in this chapter are* *perfect for a midweek supper; they take a minimum amount of time to prepare and use* *fish that is readily available.* Pasta and seafood make a delicious combination and I have *included several simple supper recipes here. Both* Spaghetti Vongole *and* Pasta with Mussels in Herb Sauce *take only minutes to prepare, and* Pasta with Smoked Salmon *offers another quick dish for a special treat.*

*The lighter recipes, such as* Spanish Style Prawns *and* Steamed Mussels with Ginger and Coriander, *make great light lunches and, again, are simple to make and ready to eat in minutes.*

# CONTENTS

≋

# SEAFOOD PIZZA

*Serves 2*

These individual pizzas, topped with mixed
seafood, taste as tantalising as they look. Served
with a crisp green salad they make the perfect
supper dish.

≈≈

*225 g/8 oz strong plain flour*
*½ tsp easy-blend yeast*
*¼ tsp salt*
*100 ml/3½ fl oz tepid water*
*1 tbsp olive oil*

**SAUCE**

*1 tbsp olive oil*
*1 garlic clove, chopped*
*4 large tomatoes, peeled,*
*seeded and chopped*
*1 tbsp tomato purée*
*2 tsp chopped fresh oregano*
*2 tsp chopped fresh basil*

**TOPPING**

*50 g/2 oz can anchovies in*
*oil, drained*
*Milk, for soaking*
*12 fresh mussels, scrubbed*
*1 tbsp olive oil*
*10 raw Mediterranean prawns,*
*shelled and de-veined (see*
*pages 6-7)*
*2 small squid, cleaned (see*
*pages 6-7), sliced into rings*
*225 g/8 oz mozzarella*
*cheese, thinly sliced*
*10 black olives*
*A few basil leaves, shredded*
*Basil sprigs, to garnish*

Make the pizza dough: combine the flour, yeast and salt
in a large bowl. Make a well in the centre, and work in
the water and oil to form a firm dough. Transfer to a
lightly floured surface, and knead for 8-10 minutes until
smooth and elastic. Place the dough in an oiled bowl,
cover and leave to rise in a warm place for 45 minutes, or
until doubled in size.

Meanwhile, prepare the sauce: heat the oil in a small
pan, fry the garlic for 2 minutes until golden, then add
the remaining ingredients. Bring to the boil, cover and
simmer gently for 15 minutes. Remove the lid, and
simmer for a further 10 minutes until thickened. Leave to
cool.

Prepare the topping: soak the anchovies in milk for 10
minutes. Drain, wash well and pat dry.

Steam the mussels in a little water for 3-4 minutes until
the shells have opened. Discard any that remain closed.
Cool slightly, and remove from their shells, reserving 4
for garnish.

Heat the oil in a large pan, and quickly fry the prawns
and squid for 1 minute until lightly browned.

Preheat the oven to 240°C/475°F/gas mark 9 and
lightly oil two 20 cm/8 in shallow cake tins. Place a large
baking sheet on the top shelf of the oven.

Knock back the risen dough, divide in half, and roll
each one into a round to fit into the prepared tins. Spread
each round with a little tomato sauce, and top with the
sliced mozzarella, prepared seafood, olives, and a few
basil leaves.

Transfer to the hot baking sheets, and cook for 18-20
minutes until risen and golden. Serve immediately, garnished with the reserved mussels, and sprigs of basil.

# SMOKED HADDOCK PILAF

*Serves 6 - 8*

Rice and fish make a great combination, and the two work well together in this spicy Middle Eastern pilaf.

| | |
|---|---|
| 450 g/1 lb smoked haddock fillets | ½ tsp ground mixed spice |
| 600 ml/1 pint Court Bouillon (see pages 6-7) | 50 g/2 oz raisins |
| | 50 g/2 oz cashew nuts, toasted |
| 225 g/8 oz basmati rice | 1 tbsp chopped fresh mint |
| 1 tsp salt | 25 g/1 oz butter (optional) |
| 2 tbsp olive oil | Pepper |
| 225 g/8 oz baby onions, halved if large | **GARNISH** |
| 1 tsp ground coriander | 2 hard-boiled eggs, quartered |
| ½ tsp ground cumin | Mint sprigs |

Wash and dry the haddock. Place in a large wide pan with the court bouillon, and bring to the boil. Simmer for about 3 minutes, until the fish starts to flake. Remove the fish with a slotted spoon, and drain on kitchen towels. Discard the skin and any bones, and flake the flesh. Reserve the stock.

Meanwhile, place the rice into a bowl with the salt. Cover with warm water, leave to cool, and then drain.

Preheat the oven to 200°C/400°F/gas mark 6, and lightly oil a large baking dish.

Fry the onions in the olive oil for 5 minutes, add the rice and spices, and stir-fry for 2 minutes.

Reheat the fish stock until boiling, and stir into the rice with the raisins and nuts. Bring to the boil, cover and simmer for 12 minutes, until the rice has absorbed most of the liquid. Stir in the mint, and remove from the heat.

Spoon one third of the rice mixture into the baking dish, arrange half of the flaked haddock over the top and repeat, finishing with the rice. Cover with foil, and bake for 20 minutes. Stir in the butter, garnish and serve.

# BAKED MACKEREL WITH LEMONS AND SPICES

*Serves 4*

A Middle Eastern-style dish, in which the lemon and spices complement the richness of the fish.

| | |
|---|---|
| 4 medium mackerel, cleaned | 4 tbsp olive oil |
| 2 lemons, sliced | 1 tsp paprika |
| 2 sprigs rosemary, bruised | Pinch of cayenne pepper |
| 4 sprigs thyme, bruised | **TO SERVE** |
| 1 tbsp dried oregano | Crisp French bread |
| 4 garlic cloves, halved | Natural yogurt |

Preheat the oven to 220°C/425°F/gas mark 7. Wash and dry the mackerel, removing the head and tails, if wished. Season the insides.

Arrange half the lemon slices, half the herbs and half the garlic cloves in the bottom of a large roasting pan. Lay the mackerel on top in a single layer, and cover with the remaining lemon slices, herbs and garlic.

Blend the oil and spices together, pour over the fish, and transfer to the oven for 20 minutes until cooked through.

Serve the mackerel with the pan juices, a spoonful of yogurt, and crisp French bread.

*Top:* BAKED MACKEREL WITH LEMONS AND SPICES
*Bottom:* SMOKED HADDOCK PILAF

# SWEET POTATO AND SALMON FISH CAKES

*Serves 6*

The sweet potatoes add an exotic flavour to this dish.

| | |
|---|---|
| *450 g/1 lb salmon fillet, skinned* | *100 g/4 oz fresh white breadcrumbs* |
| *450 g/1 lb sweet potatoes, cubed* | *4 tbsp vegetable oil* |
| *15 g/½ oz butter* | **TOMATO SAUCE** |
| *8 spring onions, chopped* | *1 tbsp olive oil* |
| *1 garlic clove, crushed* | *4 shallots, finely chopped* |
| *1 fresh green chilli, seeded and chopped* | *2 tsp chopped fresh thyme* |
| *2 tbsp chopped fresh coriander* | *450 g/1 lb ripe tomatoes, peeled, seeded and diced* |
| *1 tsp ground cumin* | *6 tbsp water* |
| *2 eggs, lightly beaten* | *2 tsp red wine vinegar* |
| *4 tbsp seasoned flour* | *Pinch of sugar* |
| | *Salt and pepper* |

Poach the salmon in cold water (see page 94). Cook the sweet potatoes in boiling water for 10-12 minutes until tender, drain well, and mash with a fork. Set aside to cool.

Meanwhile, melt the butter in a frying pan, and fry the spring onions, garlic and chilli for 5 minutes. Stir into the mashed potato with the coriander, cumin, and seasoning.

Remove the fish from its liquid, and pat dry. Flake the flesh and beat into the potato mixture with half the beaten egg until combined. Cover and chill for 1 hour.

Make the sauce: heat the olive oil in a pan, and fry the shallots for 5 minutes, stir in all the remaining ingredients, and simmer gently for a further 15 minutes. Purée in a blender until smooth, return to the pan, and keep warm.

Shape the fish mixture into 12 rounds, and flatten each one. Dust with a little seasoned flour, and dip firstly in the remaining beaten egg and then in the breadcrumbs.

Heat the vegetable oil in a frying pan, and shallow fry the fish cakes for 3-4 minutes on each side until crisp and golden. Drain on kitchen paper, and serve with the sauce.

# SMOKED HADDOCK HASH

*Serves 2*

A variation of the classic corned beef hash, this one is made with fish.and is truly scrumptious.

| | |
|---|---|
| *450 g/1 lb potatoes, cubed* | *50 g/2 oz Cheddar cheese, grated* |
| *25 g/1 oz butter* | *1 tbsp natural yogurt* |
| *1 red onion, chopped* | *1 tbsp wholegrain mustard* |
| *1 tsp chopped fresh rosemary* | *dash of tabasco sauce* |
| *1 tsp chopped fresh thyme* | |
| *225 g/8 oz smoked haddock fillet, skinned and cubed* | |

Boil the potatoes for 10-12 minutes until cooked, drain well, and mash roughly.

Melt the butter in a non-stick frying pan, and fry the onion and herbs for 5 minutes. Add the haddock, and fry for a further 2-3 minutes until the fish is opaque.

Add the mashed potato with all the remaining ingredients, and stir until evenly combined. Spread the mixture flat to the sides of the pan, and cook over a medium heat for 6-8 minutes until any liquid has evaporated, and the underside of the hash is browned.

Remove from the heat, and loosen the sides and bottom with a spatula. Place an up-turned plate over the frying pan, flip over to invert the hash, and serve at once.

*Top:* SMOKED HADDOCK HASH
*Bottom:* SWEET POTATO AND SALMON FISH CAKES

# PLAICE FILLETS WITH HERB SAUCE

*Serves 4*

A very light summer dish. To make the thyme-scented oil, simply bruise 4 sprigs of thyme, cover with 600 ml/1 pint extra virgin olive oil and leave to infuse for several days. Alternatively, simply use a good-quality extra virgin olive oil.

| | |
|---|---|
| 3 large plaice, skinned and filleted | 4 tbsp dry white wine |
| 1 tbsp thyme-scented oil (see recipe introduction) | 300 ml/½ pint Fish Stock (see pages 6-7) |
| 50 g/2 oz mixed fresh herbs (basil, chervil, chives, dill, parsley) | 50 g/2 oz mixed salad leaves |

Cut each fillet in half lengthways, season, and brush with the thyme oil. Roll up each fillet and secure with cocktail sticks.

Place the herbs in a wide pan, add the wine and stock, and arrange the plaice rolls on top. Bring to the boil, cover and steam for 8-10 minutes until the fish is cooked through. Transfer the fish to a plate, and keep warm.

Purée the herbs and pan juices until very smooth. Pour into a clean pan, bring to the boil, and simmer until reduced by half.

Toss the salad leaves with a little more scented oil, and place in the centre of 4 warmed plates. Arrange 3 plaice rolls on each plate, pour over the sauce and serve at once.

# PASTA WITH SMOKED SALMON

*Serves 4*

The age-old classic combination of smoked salmon and soured cream is a fabulous addition to fresh pasta.

| | |
|---|---|
| 25 g/1 oz unsalted butter | 350 g/12 oz smoked salmon, cut into thin strips |
| 4 shallots, chopped | |
| Grated rind of 1 lemon | 4 tbsp chopped fresh chervil |
| 2 tbsp drained capers, washed and chopped | 4 tbsp soured cream |
| | ¼ tsp freshly grated nutmeg |
| 450 g/1 lb fresh fettucine or tagliatelle | Salmon (red) caviar, to garnish (optional) |

Heat the butter in a large frying pan, and fry the shallots, lemon rind and capers for 3 minutes. Remove from the heat. Meanwhile, bring a large pan of water to the boil, and add the salt. Plunge the pasta into the boiling water, return to the boil, and simmer fast for 2 minutes until the pasta is al dente. Strain, reserving 4 tablespoons of the cooking liquid.

Return the frying pan to the heat, and stir in the pasta, reserved cooking liquid, smoked salmon, chervil, soured cream and nutmeg.

Reheat for 2 minutes, and serve at once, garnished with the salmon caviar, if wished.

*Top Right:* PLAICE FILLETS WITH HERB SAUCE
*Bottom Left:* PASTA WITH SMOKED SALMON

# RED MULLET NICOISE EN PAPILLOTE

*Serves 6*

This is my version of a classic recipe for red mullet served with a Niçoise sauce. Here the fish are baked in parchment paper to keep them moist and tender. Ask your fishmonger to prepare the red mullet.

| | |
|---|---|
| 2 tbsp olive oil | 2 tbsp capers, drained and |
| 1 red onion, finely chopped | chopped |
| 1 garlic clove, crushed | 25 g/1 oz pitted black olives, |
| 450 g/1 lb ripe tomatoes, | halved |
| peeled, seeded and diced | Salt and pepper |
| 2 tsp chopped fresh thyme | 25 g/1 oz butter, melted |
| 1 tsp dried oregano | 3 x 350 g/12 oz red mullet, |
| 2 tbsp red wine | scaled, cleaned and filleted (see |
| 4 anchovy fillets in oil, drained | recipe introduction) |
| and chopped | |

Heat the oil in a saucepan, and fry the onion and garlic for 5 minutes until browned. Add the tomatoes, thyme, oregano and red wine. Bring to the boil, and simmer for 30 minutes.

Stir in the anchovies, capers and olives. Remove from the heat, season to taste, then set aside to cool.

Preheat the oven to 190°C/375°F/gas mark 5. Cut out 6 large heart shapes from baking parchment, and make a fold down the centre of each one.

Brush one half of each heart with a little melted butter. Spoon over a little of the sauce and place a fillet of mullet on top. Fold the other half of paper over to enclose the filling, turning the edges under to seal the parcel.

Brush each parcel with the remaining butter, and transfer to a large baking sheet. Bake for 15 minutes, open 1 parcel to test if the fish is cooked, and serve straight from the parcels.

# COD FILLETS WITH SPICED CRUST

*Serves 4*

Wrapping the cod fillets with spinach leaves keeps the fish tender and moist, while the spicy crust becomes crisp and golden.

| | |
|---|---|
| 4 x 150 g/5 oz cod fillets | ½ tsp cumin seeds |
| 4 ripe tomatoes, sliced | ¼ tsp ground cinnamon |
| 8 large spinach leaves, washed | 50 g/2 oz fresh breadcrumbs |
| 4 sun-dried tomatoes in oil, | 25 g/1 oz hazelnuts, toasted |
| drained and finely chopped | and ground |
| 1 garlic clove, crushed | 1 tbsp chopped fresh parsley |
| Grated rind and juice of | 1 egg, separated |
| ½ lemon | 1 tbsp water |
| 1 tsp ground coriander | Salt and pepper |

Preheat the oven to 200°C/400°F/gas mark 6. Wash the cod fillets and pat dry. Season well, and top each with tomato slices.

Blanch the spinach leaves in boiling water for 10 seconds until just wilted. Drain, refresh under cold water, and pat dry. Wrap 2 leaves around each cod fillet.

Prepare the crust: in a bowl mix together the sun-dried tomatoes, garlic, lemon rind and juice, spices, bread-crumbs, nuts and parsley. Work in the egg yolk and water to form a soft paste.

Lightly beat the egg white, and brush the top of each spinach parcel. Divide the crust mixture into four. Spread a quarter of the mixture over each parcel, pressing down firmly, to form a thin layer over the top of each one. Brush with a little more egg white and transfer to a baking dish. Bake for 20-25 minutes, until a skewer inserted in the fish comes out hot.

Brown the crust under a hot grill, if wished, and serve at once, with a selection of steamed vegetables.

*Top:* COD FILLETS WITH SPICED CRUST
*Bottom:* RED MULLET NICOISE EN PAPILLOTE

# MONKFISH WITH BROCCOLI IN BLACK BEAN SAUCE

*Serves 4*

A quick and very tasty supper dish. Monkfish is particularly good for this dish, as its firm flesh does not fall apart during the cooking process.

| | |
|---|---|
| *450 g/1 lb skinned monkfish fillet* | *225 g/8 oz broccoli florets* |
| *1 tbsp dark soy sauce* | *120 ml/4 fl oz vegetable stock or Fish Stock (see pages 6-7)* |
| *1 tbsp lime juice* | *2 tbsp black bean sauce* |
| *2 tbsp sweet sherry* | *1 tsp clear honey* |
| *1 garlic clove, crushed* | *1 tsp cornflour* |
| *1 tsp grated fresh root ginger* | *1 tbsp sunflower oil* |
| *1 small fresh red chilli, seeded and sliced* | *1 tsp sesame oil* |

Cut the monkfish into thin slices, and place in a shallow dish. Mix together the soy sauce, lime juice, sherry, garlic, ginger and chilli. Pour over the fish, cover and marinate for 2-4 hours.

Trim the broccoli, cutting the florets in half if large. Blanch in boiling salted water for 1 minute, drain, refresh under cold water, and pat dry.

Pour the marinade juices into a bowl, and stir in the stock, black bean sauce, honey and cornflour.

Heat the 2 oils in a non-stick wok or large frying pan until it starts to smoke. Pat dry the monkfish, and stir-fry for 2 minutes until lightly browned. Add the broccoli, and stir-fry for 2 minutes. Stir in the black bean sauce mixture, and simmer for 3-4 minutes until the broccoli and fish are cooked through. Serve immediately with egg noodles or fragrant Thai rice.

# STEAMED MUSSELS WITH GINGER AND CORIANDER

*Serves 4*

A fragrant broth, infused with ginger and coriander, sets off the rich flavour of the mussels in this quick and easy supper dish.

| | |
|---|---|
| *300 ml/½ pint dry sherry* | *1 tsp grated fresh root ginger* |
| *300 ml/½ pint water* | *1 garlic clove, crushed* |
| *1 small onion, chopped* | *1 fresh green chilli, seeded and chopped* |
| *1 small carrot, chopped* | *1 leek, trimmed and shredded* |
| *1 tsp coriander seeds* | *2 carrots, cut into julienne* |
| *2 slices fresh root ginger* | *Juice of 1 lime* |
| *1 garlic clove* | *Salt and pepper* |
| *2 coriander stalks* | **GARNISH** |
| *2 kg/4½ lb mussels, scrubbed* | *2 tbsp chopped fresh coriander* |
| **SAUCE** | *Grated rind of 1 lime* |
| *1 tbsp sunflower oil* | |
| *1 tsp sesame oil* | |

To make the stock, place all the ingredients except the mussels in a large pan, bring to the boil, and simmer gently for 30 minutes. Strain the liquid into a clean pan, and boil rapidly until reduced to 150 ml/¼ pint.

Prepare the sauce: heat the sunflower and sesame oil together in a large pan, add the ginger, garlic and chilli, and fry for 3 minutes, then add the leek and carrots.

Add the reduced stock, and bring to the boil. Add the mussels, cover and cook for 6-8 minutes until all the mussels are opened, discarding any that remain closed.

Transfer to a large warmed serving dish, sprinkle over the coriander and lime, and serve immediately.

*Top:* STEAMED MUSSELS WITH GINGER AND CORIANDER
*Bottom:* MONKFISH WITH BROCCOLI IN BLACK BEAN SAUCE

## GRILLED STUFFED SARDINES

*Serves 4 - 6*

Fresh sardines, one of the most magical of all fish, are served here with a delicious spiced filling.

≈≈≈

| | |
|---|---|
| *100 g/4 oz trimmed spinach* | *50 g/2 oz fresh breadcrumbs* |
| *leaves, washed* | *50 g/2 oz feta cheese,* |
| *1 garlic clove, crushed* | *crumbled* |
| *Grated rind of 1 lemon* | *¼ tsp gound mixed spice* |
| *2 tbsp chopped fresh parsley* | *2 tbsp olive oil* |
| *25 g/1 oz pine nuts, toasted* | *12 large fresh sardines (about* |
| *and chopped* | *100 g/4 oz each), scaled and* |
| *25 g/1 oz raisins* | *cleaned* |
| *25 g/1 oz drained anchovy* | *Salt and pepper* |
| *fillets in oil, chopped* | *Lemon wedges, to garnish* |

≈≈≈

Place the washed spinach leaves in a pan with no extra water, and heat for 2-3 minutes until just wilted. Drain, squeeze out excess liquid, and chop finely.

Place the spinach in a bowl, and stir in the garlic, lemon rind, parsley, pine nuts, raisins, anchovies, bread-crumbs, feta, spice, and half the oil. Set aside for 1 hour for the flavours to infuse.

Preheat the grill. Wash and dry the sardines, and fill the stomach cavities with the spinach mixture. Brush with the remaining oil and grill for 4-5 minutes on each side until browned and firm to the touch. Serve at once with lemon wedges.

## SPANISH-STYLE PRAWNS

*Serves 4 - 6*

The addition of ground almonds to this classic Spanish dish of fried prawns, adds a rich nutty flavour.

| | |
|---|---|
| *900 g/2 lb raw Mediterranean* | *Grated rind and juice of* |
| *(king) prawns* | *1 lemon* |
| *4 tbsp olive oil* | *25 g/1 oz ground almonds,* |
| *4 garlic cloves, chopped* | *toasted* |
| *2 small dried red chillies,* | *4 tbsp chopped fresh parsley* |
| *seeded and chopped* | *Salt and pepper* |

≈≈≈

Wash and dry the prawns, but leave the head and shells intact.

Heat the oil in a large pan, and fry the garlic, chilli and lemon rind for 1 minute until just starting to turn golden. Add the prawns and stir-fry over a medium heat for 2 minutes, then cover and simmer for 4-5 minutes until cooked through.

Remove the pan from the heat, and stir in the almonds, parsley and lemon juice, season well, and serve.

*Top Left:* SPANISH-STYLE PRAWNS
*Bottom Right:* GRILLED STUFFED SARDINES

# TANDOORI FISH KEBABS

*Serves 4*

A combination of fish and prawns is marinated in spicy yogurt and then grilled to make tangy tandoori kebabs.

| | |
|---|---|
| 2 plaice, skinned and filleted | 1 tsp mild curry powder |
| 16 raw Mediterranean (king) prawns | 1 tsp paprika |
| | ¼ tsp chilli powder |
| 450 g/1 lb cod fillet, skinned | ¼ tsp turmeric |
| 2 limes, cut into wedges | 1 tbsp lemon juice |
| **MARINADE** | 150 ml/¼ pint thick natural yogurt |
| 1 small onion, very finely chopped | Salt and pepper |
| 2 garlic cloves, crushed | Lime wedges, to garnish |
| 1 tsp grated fresh root ginger | |

Wash and dry the plaice fillets. Cut each one in half lengthways to make 16 thin strips of fish. Roll up, and secure with cocktail sticks. Peel and de-vein the prawns, cut the cod fillet into cubes, and place all the fish in a shallow dish.

Combine all the marinade ingredients together, and pour over the seafood. Cover and marinate for 30 minutes. Soak 8 bamboo skewers in cold water for 30 minutes, drain and pat dry.

Preheat the grill. Thread the fish, prawns and lime wedges alternately onto the bamboo skewers. Grill for 8-10 minutes, turning and basting, until charred and cooked through.

Place 2 kebabs on each plate, garnish with lime wedges, and serve with a green salad and naan bread.

# GRILLED SALMON STEAKS

*Serves 4*

The thick Chinese-style barbecue sauce makes a fragrant golden glaze for the salmon.

| | |
|---|---|
| 2 tbsp hoisin sauce | 1 tsp grated fresh root ginger |
| 2 tbsp dark soy sauce | 4 x 150 g/5 oz salmon steaks, washed and dried |
| 1 tsp sesame oil | |
| ¼ tsp five spice powder | **TO SERVE** |
| 2 tsp clear honey | Garlic bread |
| 1 garlic clove, crushed | Mixed salad |

Place all the ingredients except the salmon in a small bowl, and stir well until combined.

Preheat the grill. Brush each salmon steak with the glaze, and grill for 3-4 minutes on each side, basting with the remaining glaze until golden and cooked through.

Serve at once with garlic bread and a mixed salad.

*Top:* TANDOORI FISH KEBABS
*Bottom:* GRILLED SALMON STEAKS

# SPAGHETTI VONGOLE

*Serves 4*

A classic pasta dish using the tiny Venus clams. If fresh clams are unavailable, buy the canned ones in their shells. If all else fails, use canned shelled clams in brine.

| | |
|---|---|
| 900 g/2 lb fresh Venus clams | 4 ripe tomatoes, peeled, seeded |
| 350 g/12 oz dried spaghetti | and diced |
| 1 tsp salt | 50 g/2 oz sun-dried tomatoes |
| SAUCE | in oil, drained and sliced |
| 4 tbsp olive oil or oil from sun- | 4 tbsp chopped fresh parsley |
| dried tomatoes | Freshly grated Parmesan |
| 2 garlic cloves, sliced | cheese, to serve (optional) |
| 1 fresh red chilli, seeded and | |
| sliced | |

Scrub the clams, and rinse under cold running water for several minutes. Place in a large pan, and steam for 3-4 minutes until the shells have opened, discarding any that remain closed.

Strain off 150 ml/¼ pint of liquid, and remove the clams from their shells, if wished.

Bring a large pan of water to a rolling boil, add the salt, and plunge in the spaghetti. Return to the boil, and simmer rapidly for 10 minutes until al dente.

Meanwhile, prepare the sauce: heat the oil in a large wide pan, and fry the garlic and chilli for 1 minute. Add the fresh and dried tomatoes, and reserved clam stock. Bring to the boil, simmer for 5 minutes until thickened, then stir in the clams.

Strain the cooked pasta, toss into the sauce with the parsley, stir for 1 minute until heated through. Serve immediately with black pepper and freshly grated Parmesan cheese.

# PASTA WITH MUSSELS IN A HERB SAUCE

*Serves 4*

A truly delicious combination of flavours make this one of my favourite pasta dishes.

| | |
|---|---|
| 2 kg/4½ lb large mussels, | Grated rind and juice of ½ |
| scrubbed | lemon |
| 350 g/12 oz dried pasta | 1 garlic clove, crushed |
| shapes | 4 tbsp chopped mixed fresh |
| 1 tsp salt | herbs (e.g. chives, parsley, |
| 25 g/1 oz butter | basil, thyme) |
| 175 g/6 oz button | 2 tbsp freshly grated Parmesan |
| mushrooms, quartered | cheese |
| HERB SAUCE | 25 g/1 oz drained anchovies, |
| 75 ml/3 fl oz virgin olive oil | finely chopped |
| | Salt and pepper |

Wash the mussels in cold running water, then steam in a large pan for 5 minutes until the shells are opened, discarding any that remain closed.

Strain off and reserve 4 tablespoons of the liquid, and remove the mussels from their shells.

Bring a large pan of water to a rolling boil, add the salt and the pasta, return to the boil, and cook for 10 minutes until al dente.

Meanwhile, make the sauce: whisk together all the ingredients with the reserved mussel stock until blended. Set aside.

Melt the butter in a large wide pan, and fry the mushrooms for 5 minutes until browned. Strain the pasta, and add to the pan with the mussels and herb sauce. Toss for 1 minute until heated through, and serve at once.

*Top:* PASTA WITH MUSSELS IN A HERB SAUCE
*Bottom:* SPAGHETTI VONGOLE

# PARSNIP NESTS WITH WHITING AND BEETROOT

*Serves  4*

Mashed parsnip and potato is piped to make small nests, and filled with a sweet and savoury beetroot and whiting sauce.

| | |
|---|---|
| 675 g/1½ lb parsnips, cubed | Pinch of sugar |
| 225 g/8 oz potatoes, peeled and cubed | Pinch of salt |
| 4 tbsp walnut oil | 175 g/6 oz cooked beetroot, diced |
| 50 g/2 oz Gruyère cheese, grated | 2 tsp balsamic vinegar |
| 1 egg yolk | 350 g/12 oz whiting fillets, skinned and cubed |
| Salt and pepper | 2 tbsp chopped fresh chives |
| FILLING | Soured cream or natural yogurt, to serve |
| 2 tbsp walnut oil | Chopped fresh chives, to garnish |
| 1 onion, sliced | |
| 1 tsp caraway seeds | |

Boil the parsnips and potatoes for 12-15 minutes until cooked. Drain and mash with the oil, cheese, egg yolk and salt and pepper. Set aside to cool, then transfer to a piping bag fitted with a large star nozzle.

Meanwhile, make the filling: heat the oil in a heavy-based pan, and fry the onion with the caraway seeds, sugar and salt for 10 minutes. Add the beetroot and vinegar, cover and cook for a further 10 minutes.

Preheat the oven to 220°C/425°F/gas mark 7. Oil a large baking sheet, and pipe on four 10 cm/4 in circles of the parsnip and potato mash. Then pipe a ring around the edge of each one to form 'nests'. Bake for 15-20 minutes until golden and crisp.

Return the beetroot mixture to the heat. Add the whiting and chives, cover and cook for 6-8 minutes.

Remove the potato 'nests' from the oven, spoon in the filling, top each one with a spoonful of soured cream or yogurt and serve at once, garnished with chives.

# SEAFOOD PIE WITH POTATO CRUST

*Serves  6 - 8*

A delicious fish pie ideal for mid-week entertaining, especially as it freezes well.

| | |
|---|---|
| 2 tbsp olive oil | 225 g/8 oz smoked cod fillet |
| 2 leeks, sliced | 175 g/6 oz cooked peeled prawns |
| 3 celery stalks, sliced | ¼ tsp grated nutmeg |
| 40 g/1½ oz plain flour | POTATO |
| 150 ml/¼ pint dry cider or white wine | TOPPING |
| 300 ml/½ pint milk | 900 g/2 lb potatoes, peeled and cubed |
| 50 g/2 oz mature cheese, grated | 4 tbsp olive oil |
| 225 g/8 oz frozen leaf spinach, thawed | 2 tbsp chopped fresh thyme |
| 225 g/8 oz hake or haddock fillet | 50 g/2 oz freshly grated Parmesan cheese |
| | Salt and pepper |

Prepare the filling: heat the oil in a large pan, and fry the leeks and celery for 5 minutes. Stir in the flour, and cook for a further minute. Gradually add the cider or wine and then the milk, stirring constantly, until smooth and thickened. Bring to the boil, simmer gently for 5 minutes, then remove from the heat and stir in the cheese.

Drain the spinach, and squeeze out the excess water. Mix with the fish and prawns, and stir into the cheese sauce. Spoon into a 1.75 litre/3 pint pie dish.

Make the topping: preheat the oven to 200°C/ 400°F/gas mark 6. Cook the potatoes in boiling salted water for 12-15 minutes until tender, drain well, and mash with the oil, thyme, cheese and seasonings.

Spoon or pipe the mashed potato over the fish, and bake for 50-60 minutes until golden and bubbling. Cover with foil if the topping starts to become over brown.

*Top:* SEAFOOD PIE WITH POTATO CRUST
*Bottom:* PARSNIP NESTS WITH WHITING AND BEETROOT

# COD STEAKS WITH CITRUS SAUCE

*Serves 4*

A wonderfully light and refreshing summer dish served with a selection of vegetables. Use dill if fennel fronds are unavailable.

≈≈≈

| | |
|---|---|
| *4 x 150 g/5 oz cod steaks* | *450 g/1 lb summer vegetables* |
| *1-2 tbsp olive oil* | *(asparagus, sweetcorn, carrots,* |
| *Juice of 2 oranges* | *patty pans, courgettes, French* |
| *Juice of 1 lemon* | *beans), trimmed and sliced as* |
| *4 tbsp dry white wine* | *necessary* |
| *Grated rind of 1 orange* | *Salt and pepper* |
| *Grated rind of ½ lemon* | *4 tbsp double cream or crème* |
| *2 tbsp chopped fennel fronds* | *fraîche, to serve (optional)* |

≈≈≈

Preheat the oven to 220°C/425°F/gas mark 7. Cut 4 large sheets of foil, and brush each with a little oil. Wash and dry the fish, and place 1 steak in the centre of each sheet, pulling up the sides to form a bowl.

Mix together the orange juice, lemon juice, wine, citrus rinds and fennel, and spoon over the fish. Draw up the edges of foil, and twist together to seal the parcels. Place on a large baking sheet, and bake for 15 minutes until cod is cooked.

Meanwhile, steam the vegetables for 3-5 minutes, depending on the size, until tender. Toss with a little oil, and keep warm.

Arrange the vegetables on plates, open up the parcels, and arrange the steaks on top of the vegetables. Pour over the juices from the parcels, and serve at once, topped with a spoonful of cream or crème fraîche.

# TROUT WITH BACON, MUSHROOMS AND SAGE

*Serves 4*

A classic combination of bacon, mushrooms and sage makes a rich sauce to serve with whole grilled trout.

≈≈≈

| | |
|---|---|
| *4 x 350 g/12 oz trout,* | *1 tbsp chopped fresh sage* |
| *cleaned, heads removed if* | *120 ml/4 fl oz port* |
| *wished* | *120 ml/4 fl oz chicken or* |
| *1½ tbsp olive oil* | *vegetable stock* |
| *225 g/8 oz bacon, rinded and* | *1 tbsp balsamic vinegar* |
| *chopped* | **GARNISH** |
| *225 g/8 oz button* | *Lemon wedges* |
| *mushrooms, wiped* | *Sage leaves* |

≈≈≈

Preheat the grill. Wash and dry the trout, and season the insides. Brush with a little oil, and grill for 12-15 minutes, turning once, until the skin is browned and the fish feels firm to the touch. Keep warm.

Meanwhile, make the sauce: heat the remaining oil in a pan, and fry the bacon for 3 minutes until browned. Add the mushrooms and sage, and fry for a further 5 minutes until the mushrooms are browned.

Add the port and ignite with a match. Boil rapidly until the flames die down, then pour in the stock and vinegar. Simmer gently for 5 minutes until the sauce is thick and glossy.

Transfer the trout to warmed plates. Spoon over the sauce, and serve immediately, garnished with lemon wedges and sage leaves.

*Top:* TROUT WITH BACON, MUSHROOMS AND SAGE
*Bottom:* COD STEAKS WITH CITRUS SAUCE

# ITALIAN MIXED SEAFOOD SALAD

*Serves 4*

This is my version of the classic Italian mixed seafood salad. Use the tiny Venus clams if possible as they are sweet and tender.

| | |
|---|---|
| 350 g/12 oz small raw prawns, shelled and de-veined (see pages 6-7) | 1 red pepper, seeded and thinly sliced |
| 350 g/12 oz squid, cleaned (see page 6-7), sliced into rings | 2 celery stalks, thinly sliced |
| 300 ml/½ pint Court Bouillon (see pages 6-7) | 1 small head fennel, thinly sliced |
| 450 g/1 lb fresh mussels | 100 g/4 oz pitted green olives, halved |
| 450 g/1 lb fresh Venus clams | 2 tbsp chopped celery leaves |
| 175 ml/6 fl oz olive oil | 1 tbsp chopped fresh basil |
| 3 tbsp lemon juice | Salt and pepper |

Wash and dry the prawns and squid and place in a large pan. Add the court bouillon, bring to the boil, and simmer gently for 4-5 minutes until prawns and squid are tender. Strain the stock into a clean pan, and reserve the seafood.

Scrub the mussels and clams, and cook in the stock for 5 minutes until the shells have opened. Discard any that remain closed.

Remove the mussels and clams from their shells, and reserve the stock for another recipe.

Place all the seafood in a large bowl, and stir in the oil and lemon juice until well blended. Set aside for 2 hours.

Just before serving, stir in the remaining ingredients, and serve with crusty bread.

# SARDINES WITH CAPONATA

*Serves 4*

A great combination based on Sicilian cooking.

| | |
|---|---|
| 6 tbsp olive oil | 2 ripe tomatoes, chopped |
| 1 onion, chopped | 1½ tbsp red wine vinegar |
| 1 garlic clove, chopped | 1 tsp sugar |
| 2 celery stalks, sliced | 12 large sardines |
| 1 tbsp chopped fresh basil | Juice of 1 lemon |
| 1 medium aubergine, diced | 2 tbsp pine nuts, toasted |
| 50 g/2 oz pitted green olives, halved | Garlic Sauce (see page 32), to serve |
| 2 tbsp capers | |

Heat 2 tablespoons of the oil in a frying pan, and fry the onion, garlic, celery and basil for 5 minutes until browned. Transfer the mixture to a bowl with a slotted spoon.

Add the remaining oil to the pan, and fry the aubergines for 5-6 minutes until golden. Add to the onion and celery mixture with the olives and capers.

Place the tomatoes, vinegar and sugar in a saucepan, bring to the boil, cover and simmer gently for 15 minutes. Stir in the vegetable mixture and pine nuts, season to taste, and set aside to cool slightly.

Preheat the grill. Clean the sardines, and discard the heads and tails, if wished. Brush inside and outside with oil, season, and squeeze over a little lemon juice. Grill the fish for 4-5 minutes on each side, until charred and cooked through.

Spoon the caponata mixture onto individual serving plates, top each with 3 sardines, and serve at once with garlic sauce, if wished.

*Top:* SARDINES WITH CAPONATA
*Bottom:* ITALIAN MIXED SEAFOOD SALAD

# DINNER
# PARTY DISHES

*F*ISH AND SEAFOOD *can make some of the most impressive dinner party dishes; the recipes in this chapter tend to use more exotic fish and some are aimed at those who cook fish and seafood regularly. However not all are difficult to achieve; for example,* Monkfish Baked with Bay Leaves and Garlic *and* Whole Sea Bass Baked in Sea Salt *are both exotic and yet simple to prepare and suitable for any occasion.*

*Many recipes in this chapter do take a little more time, and some, such as the spectacular* Elegant Fish Pie, *require more skill to ensure success, but a little planning ahead goes a long way and I'm sure your guests will agree that the results are well worth that extra effort.*

# CONTENTS

# SQUID INK PASTA WITH SQUID SAUCE

*Serves 4*

Squid ink is available in packets from good fishmongers, alternatively try to buy squid with their ink sacs still intact.

≈≈≈

| | |
|---|---|
| *225 g/8 oz plain flour* | *6 tbsp olive oil* |
| *1 tsp salt* | *2 shallots, chopped* |
| *2 eggs, plus 1 egg yolk* | *2 garlic cloves, sliced* |
| *½ tsp squid ink* | *4 tbsp chopped fresh parsley* |
| *2 tbsp olive oil* | *2 tbsp drained green* |
| *1-2 tbsp water* | *peppercorns, lightly crushed* |
| **SQUID SAUCE** | *Salt and pepper* |
| *900 g/2 lb baby squid,* | |
| *cleaned (see page 00)* | |

≈≈≈

Sift the flour and salt into a large bowl. Make a well in the centre, and gradually work in the eggs, egg yolk, squid ink, olive oil, and enough water to form a firm dough. Knead on a lightly floured surface for 5 minutes until elastic, wrap and leave to rest for 30 minutes.

Divide the dough into 8 equal pieces, and using a pasta machine, roll into 8 long thin sheets. Leave to hang over a pole for 5 minutes, then pass through the tagliatelle attachment on the pasta machine. Flour a large clean tea towel, and curl the tagliatelle into piles. Set aside.

Slice the squid into rings, and the tentacles in half, if large. Wash well and pat dry.

Heat 2 tablespoons of the oil in a large frying pan, add the shallots and garlic, and fry for 2 minutes until softened and lightly golden. Add the squid rings and tentacles, and stir-fry over a high heat for 2-3 minutes. Add the parsley and peppercorns to the squid mixture and stir well.

Meanwhile, bring a large pan of water to the boil. Add 2 teaspoons of salt and plunge in the pasta. Return to the boil, and cook for 2-3 minutes until al dente. Drain, and stir into the squid pan with the remaining oil. Stir over a high heat for 1 minute, and serve at once.

# BAKED SEA BASS WITH FENNEL AND ROCKET

*Serves 6*

The flavours of sea bass and fennel combine to make a wonderful dish. Ask your fishmonger to fillet three small sea bass for you.

≈≈≈

| | |
|---|---|
| *6 x 225 g/8 oz sea bass fillets* | *6 tbsp dry white wine* |
| *1 onion, sliced* | *2 heads fennel* |
| *1 lemon, sliced* | *3 tbsp walnut oil* |
| *1 tbsp fennel seeds* | *350 g/12 oz rocket* |
| *1 tsp white peppercorns* | *Freshly grated nutmeg* |
| *4 sprigs thyme* | *Salt and pepper* |
| *2 sprigs rosemary* | |

≈≈≈

Preheat the oven to 220°C/425°F/gas mark 7, and line a roasting pan with foil.

Wash and dry the bass, and pull out any small bones that remain.

Place the onion slices, lemon slices, fennel seeds, peppercorns, herbs and wine in the prepared tin. Arrange the fillets on top, skin-side up.

Cover the tin with a second piece of foil, and bake the fish for about 20 minutes, or until cooked through.

Meanwhile, preheat the grill. Cut the fennel lengthways into thin slices, brush with a little of the oil, and grill for 6-8 minutes on each side, until golden and tender. Keep warm.

Just before serving, heat the remaining oil in a pan. Add the rocket, and cook for 1 minute, stirring, until just wilted. Season with nutmeg, and salt and pepper.

Transfer the rocket to warmed plates. Top with the grilled fennel, and arrange a fillet of sea bass on each one. Serve at once, garnished with baked onion slices, fennel seeds and rosemary from the first baking.

*Top:* SQUID INK PASTA WITH SQUID SAUCE
*Bottom:* BAKED SEA BASS WITH FENNEL AND ROCKET

## RED SNAPPER CREOLE

*Serves 4*

This fiery red sauce is typical of Creole cookery, and keeps the fish beautifully moist as it bakes. Substitute other exotic fish, such as parrot fish, red mullet or daurade, if snapper are unavailable.

| | |
|---|---|
| *4 red snapper (about 350 g/* | *2 garlic cloves, crushed* |
| *12 oz each), scaled and* | *1 tbsp chopped fresh thyme* |
| *cleaned* | *450 g/1 lb ripe tomatoes,* |
| *Salt and pepper* | *peeled, seeded and chopped* |
| *2 tbsp olive oil* | *300 ml/½ pint vegetable stock* |
| *1 onion, sliced* | *1-2 tbsp chilli sauce* |
| *2 red peppers, seeded and* | *1 tsp sugar* |
| *chopped* | *2 tbsp chopped fresh coriander* |

Wash and dry the snapper, and season inside and out with salt and pepper. Set aside.

Heat the oil in a large saucepan, and fry the onion, pepper, garlic and thyme for 5 minutes. Add the tomatoes, stock, chilli sauce and sugar, bring to the boil, and simmer for 20 minutes.

Preheat the oven to 200°C/400°F/gas mark 6. Spoon half the sauce into a large casserole, arrange the snapper on top, then spoon over the remaining sauce. Sprinkle with coriander, and cover and bake for 25 minutes until the snapper are cooked through.

Serve with boiled rice or bread to soak up the juices.

## ROASTED FISH WITH GARLIC AND SHALLOTS

*Serves 4*

Roasting garlic and shallots in their skins allows them to become soft, mellow and totally delicious. Ask your fishmonger to scale and clean the fish.

| | |
|---|---|
| *12 unpeeled garlic cloves* | *4 tbsp walnut or olive oil* |
| *12 unpeeled shallots* | *Sea salt and pepper* |
| *1 dried red chilli, seeded and* | *4 x 350 g/12 oz bream or red* |
| *chopped* | *mullet, scaled and cleaned (see* |
| *2 tbsp chopped fresh sage* | *recipe introduction)* |
| *4 sprigs thyme* | |

Preheat the oven to 220°C/425°F/gas mark 7. Place the garlic, shallots, chilli, herbs and oil in a large roasting pan, toss well, and sprinkle with sea salt and pepper. Bake for 20 minutes.

Add the fish, making spaces for them to fit in snugly among the vegetables. Return to the oven for 15 minutes, or until the fish are firm to the touch.

Remove the pan from the oven, cover with foil, and leave to rest for 5 minutes. Serve at once.

*Top:* RED SNAPPER CREOLE
*Bottom:* ROASTED FISH WITH GARLIC AND SHALLOTS

# CHARRED SOLE WITH MEDITERRANEAN VEGETABLES

*Serves 4*

If possible, cook the sole over a charcoal fire to get the maximum flavour. Otherwise, a grill will suffice.

| | |
|---|---|
| 2 x 450 g/1 lb lemon sole, skinned | 1 aubergine, sliced |
| 1 red onion, cut into wedges | 2 courgettes, sliced |
| 2 red peppers, seeded and quartered | 4 large flat mushrooms, quartered |
| 6 tbsp olive oil | DRESSING |
| 4 sprigs thyme | 4 tbsp olive oil |
| 2 sprigs rosemary | 1 tbsp balsamic vinegar |
| 2 garlic cloves, chopped | Pinch of sugar |
| | Salt and pepper |

Wash and dry the sole and discard the head, tail and fin bones. Cut each one in half widthways to give 4 equal-sized pieces of fish. Cover and set side.

Preheat the oven to 220°C/425°F/gas mark 7. Place the onion wedges, peppers, half of the oil, the herbs and garlic in a large roasting pan, and toss well together. Bake for 20 minutes on the top shelf of the oven.

Add the remaining vegetables, stir once, and bake for a further 20 minutes until caramelized.

Blend the dressing ingredients together, and brush a little over the sole. Cook over coals or under a grill for 6-8 minutes on each side, basting once, until charred and firm to the touch.

Warm the remaining dressing ingredients in a small pan. Arrange the vegetables on individual plates, top with the fish, pour over the dressing, and serve at once.

# MONKFISH BAKED WITH BAY LEAVES AND GARLIC

*Serves 4*

This recipe is based on a dish prepared for me when I was working in Greece. They used an eel, but I prefer to use monkfish. Ask your fishmonger to prepare the monkfish, if wished.

| | |
|---|---|
| 1 x 900 g/2 lb monkfish tail, skin and tail removed | Salt and pepper |
| 8 bay leaves | 2 tbsp olive oil |
| 1 lemon, sliced | 6 tbsp dry white wine |
| 8 garlic cloves | 1 onion, sliced |
| | 6 sprigs rosemary |

Preheat the oven to 220°C/425°F/gas mark 7. Carefully cut down each side of the monkfish bone and remove it without cutting the body completely in half.

Place the bay leaves, half the lemon slices and the garlic cloves in the centre of the fish. Season well and tie together with string, at 2.5 cm/1 in intervals.

Heat half the oil in a heavy-based, non-stick frying pan. Fry the fish for 2-3 minutes, turning, until well browned all over. Add the wine, boil for 1 minute, and remove from the heat.

Place the onion slices, remaining lemon slices and rosemary sprigs in a roasting pan. Sit the browned fish on top and pour over the pan juices. Bake for 30 minutes until a skewer inserted in the centre comes out hot.

Place the fish on a serving dish, and remove the string. Cover with foil, and leave to rest for 5 minutes before serving.

*Top:* MONKFISH BAKED WITH BAY LEAVES AND GARLIC
*Bottom:* CHARRED SOLE WITH MEDITERRANEAN VEGETABLES

# TUNA TERIYAKI WITH GLAZED TOMATOES

*Serves 4*

The fish is seared over a high heat to brown the outside, leaving the inside raw, making a delicious contrast in textures. Plunging the seared fish into cold water halts the cooking process.

| | |
|---|---|
| 1 x 450 g/1 lb tuna loin or steak | 100 ml/4 fl oz boiling water |
| 3 tbsp tamari soy sauce | 2 tbsp olive oil |
| 75 ml/3 fl oz water | 225 g/8 oz red and yellow cherry tomatoes, halved |
| 2 tbsp dry sherry | 1 tbsp clear honey |
| 1 tbsp rice or wine vinegar | Salt and pepper |
| 50 g/2 oz dried shiitake mushrooms | |

Cut the tuna loin or steak into four. Wash, pat dry and place in a shallow dish.

Blend together the soy sauce, water, sherry and rice or wine vinegar and pour over the tuna. Cover and leave to marinate for at least 2 hours.

Soak the dried mushrooms in the boiling water for 30 minutes. Drain well, reserving the liquid, and slice.

Drain the marinade from the tuna, and reserve. Heat half the oil in a heavy-based frying pan, until just starting to smoke. Dry the tuna and seal in the hot oil for 1-2 minutes, browning on all sides. Remove from the heat and immediately plunge into cold water. Pat dry.

Sear the tomato halves, cut-side down on the griddle, and set aside.

Heat the remaining oil in a small frying pan, add the mushrooms, and fry for 2 minutes. Add the reserved tuna marinade and mushroom liquid, bring to the boil, then cover and simmer for 10 minutes. Stir in the honey, add the tomatoes and simmer for 1 minute.

Cut the tuna strips into very thin slices, and serve with the caramelized tomato sauce.

# BAKED TROUT WITH THAI SPICES

*Serves 4*

The curry paste requires coriander roots for a truly authentic flavour. Bunches of fresh coriander usually come with the roots still attached, which need washing well. Alternatively, use two coriander stalks.

| | |
|---|---|
| 4 medium trout, cleaned | 4 garlic cloves, chopped |
| **RED CURRY PASTE** | 2 shallots, chopped |
| | 1 tsp ground black pepper |
| 8 dried red chillies, seeded and chopped | **SAUCE** |
| 8 coriander roots, washed and chopped | 1 bunch spring onions, sliced |
| | 4 tbsp dark soy sauce |
| 1 tbsp grated fresh root ginger | 4 tbsp dry sherry |
| 2 stalks lemon grass, chopped | 4 tbsp water |
| 4 kaffir lime leaves, shredded, or grated rind of 2 limes | Juice of 2 limes |
| | 2 tbsp chopped fresh coriander |

Preheat the oven to 200°C/400°F/gas mark 6. Wash and dry the trout, cut 4 slashes in each side.

Make the curry paste: place all the ingredients in a blender, and purée until smooth. Spread the mixture all over the inside and outside of the trout.

Lightly oil 4 sheets of foil, and place a trout in the centre of each one. Draw up the edges of the foil, leaving a gap in the top.

Combine all the sauce ingredients together, and divide between the parcels, spooning the sauce through the gaps. Seal the edges by twisting the foil over.

Place the parcels on a large baking sheet. Transfer to the oven, and bake for 20-25 minutes until the trout are cooked through. Serve at once.

*Top:* BAKED TROUT WITH THAI SPICES
*Bottom:* TUNA TERIYAKI WITH GLAZED TOMATOES

# HALIBUT WITH VERMICELLI

*Serves 6*

Based on a classic Spanish recipe, this delicious dish using dried vermicelli pasta needs to be eaten as soon as it is cooked, to prevent it from becoming dry.

| | |
|---|---|
| *6 x 150 g/5 oz halibut steaks* | *4 ripe tomatoes, peeled, seeded* |
| *900 ml/1½ pints Fish Stock* | *and diced* |
| *(see pages 6-7)* | *Pinch of saffron strands* |
| *450 ml/¾ pint tomato juice* | *1 tsp ground cumin* |
| *2 tbsp olive oil* | *Pinch cayenne pepper* |
| *4 garlic cloves, crushed* | *225 g/8 oz vermicelli, broken* |
| | *into short lengths* |

Start by poaching the fish: wash and dry the halibut steaks, and place in a large pan to fit in a single layer. Add the fish stock and tomato juice, bring to the boil, simmer for 1 minute, and remove from the heat.

Strain 900 ml/1½ pints of the stock carefully into a jug, and allow the fish to cool in the remaining stock.

Heat the oil in a large pan, and fry the garlic for 2 minutes. Add the tomatoes, and fry for 10 minutes. Stir in the saffron, spices and vermicelli, and fry for 1 minute.

Add the fish stock, bring to the boil, and simmer for 10 minutes until the vermicelli is cooked.

When the vermicelli is almost ready, gently reheat the fish in its stock. Transfer the fish to serving plates, and serve the vermicelli separately.

# GRILLED LOBSTER WITH FENNEL SAUCE

*Serves 2*

Rich and delicious, the perfect dish for a celebration. As the lobster is to be cooked twice, ask your fishmonger to undercook the lobster for you, otherwise after grilling, the meat may become tough.

| | |
|---|---|
| *2 cooked lobsters (about 450 g/* | **FENNEL SAUCE** |
| *1 lb each) (see recipe* | *150 ml/¼ pint olive oil* |
| *introduction)* | *50 ml/2 fl oz boiling water* |
| **MARINADE** | *Juice of 1 lemon* |
| *6 tbsp olive oil* | *1 garlic clove, crushed* |
| *2 garlic cloves, crushed* | *2 tbsp chopped fennel fronds* |
| *1 tbsp chopped fennel fronds* | *1 tbsp chopped fresh parsley* |
| *1 tsp dried oregano* | |

Cut the lobsters in half through the centre of their heads and bodies. Arrange cut side up in a shallow dish. Combine the marinade ingredients in a bowl, and pour over the lobsters. Cover, and leave to marinate for 1 hour.

Make the sauce: place the oil in a bowl, gradually whisk in the boiling water, and then all the remaining ingredients. Continue to whisk for 1 minute until the sauce is slightly thickened.

Preheat the grill. Baste the lobsters with a little of the fennel sauce and grill for 5-6 minutes until sizzling and golden, basting frequently.

Serve hot with the remaining sauce.

*Top:* HALIBUT WITH VERMICELLI
*Bottom:* GRILLED LOBSTER WITH FENNEL SAUCE

# ELEGANT FISH PIE

*Serves 8*

An attractive fish-shaped puff pastry pie makes a
stunning dinner party dish. If using samphire,
soak in plenty of cold water for 1 hour to
remove excess saltiness.

≈

*25 g/1 oz butter*
*1 onion, finely chopped*
*40 g/1½ oz plain flour*
*300 ml/½ pint soured cream*
*¼ tsp ground mace*
*Salt and pepper*
*350 g/12 oz sole fillets,
skinned*

*350 g/12 oz salmon fillets,
skinned*
*Grated rind and juice of 1 lime*
*175 g/6 oz samphire, soaked
and drained, or asparagus tips*
*450 g/1 lb puff pastry,
thawed if frozen*
*Beaten egg, to glaze*

Melt the butter in a pan and fry the onion for 5 minutes,
stir in the flour and cook for 1 minute. Gradually add the
cream, stirring until smooth. Cook for 2 minutes, then
remove from the heat and add the mace and seasonings.
Cover the surface with baking parchment, and leave to
cool.

Wash and dry the fish fillets, and pull out any remaining
bones. Cut the flesh into large cubes. Stir the fish into the
cooled cream sauce with the lime rind and juice. Cover
and set aside.

Preheat the oven to 220°C/425°F/gas mark 7, and
lightly oil a large baking sheet. Blanch the samphire or
asparagus tips in boiling salted water for 2 minutes. Drain,
refresh under cold water, and pat dry.

Roll out half the pastry to a large rectangle about 25 x
30 cm/10 x 12 in, and cut out a large fish shape. Transfer
to the prepared baking sheet. Roll out the remaining
pastry to a slightly larger rectangle.

Carefully arrange the samphire or asparagus and the fish
mixture over the pastry fish, leaving a 2.5 cm/1 in border
around the edges. Dampen the edges, and place the rectangle of pastry over the top, pressing the edges together
well to seal. Trim the top layer to match the base, knock
up and flute the edges.

Mark scale and fin shapes over the pastry with a small
knife, and brush with the beaten egg. Bake for 20
minutes, then lower the oven temperature to 190°C/
375°F/gas mark 5, and bake for a further 10-15 minutes
until the pastry is risen and golden, and a skewer inserted
in the centre comes out hot.

# SMOKED SALMON AND POTATO TORTE

*Serves 8 - 10*

Layers of thinly sliced potato and smoked salmon are baked in a cake tin to make a really fabulous pie.

≈≈≈

| | |
|---|---|
| *2 tbsp olive oil* | *225 g/8 oz ricotta or low-fat* |
| *675 g/1½ lb potatoes* | *curd cheese* |
| *Pepper* | *1 garlic clove, crushed* |
| *350 g/12 oz smoked salmon* | *1 tbsp chopped fresh dill* |
| | *6 ripe tomatoes, thinly sliced* |

≈≈≈

Preheat the oven to 220°C/425°F/gas mark 7, and lightly oil a 23 cm/9 in spring-release tin.

Cut the potatoes into wafer thin slices, using a sharp knife or food processor fitted with the slicing blade.

Arrange a single layer of potato slices over the base of the prepared tin, season with pepper, and top with a layer of smoked salmon.

Beat the cheese, garlic and dill together. Carefully spread one-third of the mixture over the smoked salmon. Arrange a layer of tomato slices over the cheese. Repeat all the layers, finishing with a final layer of potato.

Pour over the remaining oil, and bake for about 1 hour until the potatoes are golden, and a skewer inserted in the centre comes out hot. Cover the torte with foil if it starts to burn.

Remove from the oven, and allow to cool in the tin for 5 minutes. Unmould the torte, and using a very sharp knife, cut into wedges to serve.

# SALMON FILO PARCELS WITH ROCKET PESTO

*Serves 4*

The peppery rocket mellows as it cooks inside the filo parcels, giving a delicate and delicious sauce for the salmon.

≈≈≈

| | |
|---|---|
| *4 x 100 g/4 oz salmon fillets, skinned* | *Grated rind and juice of ½ lemon* |
| *8 small sheets of filo pastry, thawed if frozen* | *1 garlic clove, crushed* |
| *4 tbsp olive oil* | *25 g/1 oz pine nuts, toasted* |
| **ROCKET PESTO** | *50 g/2 oz low-fat cream cheese* |
| *100 g/4 oz rocket leaves* | *Salt and pepper* |
| *2 juniper berries, crushed* | |

≈≈≈

Preheat the oven to 220°C/425°F/gas mark 7, and lightly oil a baking sheet.

Start by making the pesto: place all the ingredients in a blender and purée to form a fairly smooth paste. Adjust the seasoning, cover and set aside.

Wash and pat dry the salmon fillets, and pull out any remaining bones.

Brush each sheet of filo pastry with oil. Place 2 sheets together and sit a salmon fillet in the centre. Spread a quarter of the pesto over each salmon fillet. Carefully fold over the pastry to enclose the filling and seal the parcel. Brush with oil, and transfer to the baking sheet. Repeat to make 4 parcels.

Bake for 20-25 minutes until the pastry is crisp and golden. Serve with asparagus or a salad.

*Top:* SMOKED SALMON AND POTATO TORTE
*Bottom:* SALMON FILO PARCELS WITH ROCKET PESTO

# WHOLE SEA BASS BAKED IN SEA SALT

*Serves 4*

The sight of this magnificent fish in a golden crust of sea salt is sure to bring gasps of appreciation from your dinner guests. The fish cooks slowly in its blanket of salt, which comes away easily once cooked, leaving a succulent and quite delicious fish underneath.

≈

| | |
|---|---|
| *1 x 2 kg/4 lb sea bass, scaled and cleaned* | *2 whole garlic cloves* |
| *2 sprigs thyme* | *Salt and pepper* |
| *2 sprigs parsley* | *450 g/1 lb sea salt* |
| *½ lemon, sliced* | *4 egg whites* |
| | *Lemon wedges, to serve* |

≈

Preheat the oven to 190°C/375°F/gas mark 5. Wash and dry the bass. Stuff the stomach cavity with the herbs, lemon slices, garlic and seasonings.

Place the sea salt in a bowl. Lightly whisk the egg whites until frothy, then stir into the salt until mixed.

Oil a large, narrow baking dish and place the fish into it. Spread over the sea salt mixture to completely coat the bass. Transfer to the oven, and bake for 40 minutes until the salt is golden.

Remove from the oven, and leave to rest for 10 minutes. Break open the salt covering, and serve the fish with lemon wedges.

# DOVER SOLE WITH FRESH HERB SAUCE

*Serves 2*

Dover sole has such a superlative flavour that simple grilling is my favourite cooking method; a fresh-tasting herb sauce, the perfect accompaniment.

≈

| | |
|---|---|
| *2 Dover sole, cleaned and skinned* | *150 ml/¼ pint Fish Stock (see pages 6-7)* |
| *Olive oil, for brushing* | *4 tbsp chopped fresh herbs* |
| *25 g/1 oz butter* | *2 tbsp drained capers* |
| *2 shallots* | *Grated rind of 1 lemon* |
| *150 ml/¼ pint dry white wine* | *50 g/2 oz unsalted butter* |

≈

Wash and dry the fish, and brush liberally with olive oil. Preheat the grill.

Meanwhile, melt the butter in a small pan, and fry the shallots for 3 minutes until softened but not browned. Add the wine and stock, and boil rapidly until the sauce is reduced by half.

Place the fish under the grill, and cook for 6-8 minutes on each side until firm to the touch.

While the fish is cooking, add the herbs, capers and lemon rind to the wine sauce. Simmer, covered, for 5 minutes. Whisk in the butter, a little at a time, until the sauce is glossy. Keep warm.

Arrange the sole on serving plates, and pour over the herb sauce. Serve at once, garnished with fresh herbs, and accompanied by steamed vegetables and sautéed potatoes.

*Top:* WHOLE SEA BASS BAKED IN SALT
*Bottom:* DOVER SOLE WITH FRESH HERB SAUCE

## PRAWN AND FENNEL RISOTTO

*Serves 6*

A delicious creamy risotto,
ideal for a winter evening.

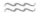

| | |
|---|---|
| *675 g / 1½ lb small raw* | *350 g / 12 oz arborio rice* |
| *Mediterranean prawns* | *150 ml / ¼ pint white wine* |
| *1.5 litres / 2½ pints water* | *2 ripe tomatoes, peeled, seeded* |
| *Pinch of saffron strands* | *and diced* |
| *3 tbsp olive oil* | *2 tbsp chopped fresh dill* |
| *1 onion, chopped* | *50 g / 2 oz soft goat cheese* |
| *2 garlic cloves, crushed* | *Salt and pepper* |
| *1 head fennel, trimmed and* | *Freshly grated Parmesan* |
| *diced* | *cheese, to serve (optional)* |

Peel and de-vein the prawns (see pages 6-7). Place the heads and shells in a pan with the cold water and a pinch of salt. Bring to the boil, skim the surface, and simmer gently for 20 minutes.

Strain the liquid through a fine sieve into a clean pan. Boil rapidly until reduced to about 900 ml/1½ pints. Add the saffron strands, and set aside to infuse.

Heat the oil in a large heavy-based pan, and fry the onion, garlic and fennel for 5 minutes. Add the rice, and stir-fry for 2 minutes.

Add the wine and boil rapidly until almost evaporated. Add about 150 ml/¼ pint of the saffron stock, and simmer until absorbed. Continue adding the stock, a little at a time, and stirring frequently, until almost all the liquid is used up (about 25 minutes).

Stir the prawns into the pan with the remaining stock and cook for 6-8 minutes, until the prawns are pink.

Stir in the remaining ingredients and heat through. Season to taste and serve at once with some freshly grated Parmesan, if wished.

## SWORDFISH KEBABS WITH PUY LENTILS

*Serves 4*

If you cannot find Puy lentils, use
brown lentils instead.

| | |
|---|---|
| *100 g / 4 oz Puy lentils* | *2 tbsp chopped fresh basil* |
| *7 tbsp olive oil* | *50 g / 2 oz pitted black olives,* |
| *1 red onion, diced* | *chopped* |
| *1 small red pepper, seeded and* | *675 g / 1½ lb fresh swordfish* |
| *diced* | *steak, cubed* |
| *1 garlic clove, crushed* | *Salt and pepper* |
| *Juice of 1 lemon* | |

Soak the lentils in cold water for 4 hours.

Drain the lentils well, place in a pan, and cover with cold water. Bring to the boil, simmer gently for 35-40 minutes until tender, then drain.

Heat 2 tablespoons of the oil in a frying pan, and fry the onion, pepper and garlic for 5 minutes. Add the lemon juice, lentils, basil and olives, and simmer gently for 3 minutes. Keep warm.

Preheat the grill. Thread the cubed swordfish onto 8 small skewers. Brush with a little of the remaining oil, and place under the grill. Cook for 4-5 minutes, turning and basting, until golden and firm to the touch.

Stir the remaining oil into the lentil mixture, and heat through. Spoon onto warmed plates and top with the brochettes. Serve at once with a crisp green salad.

*Top Right:* SWORDFISH KEBABS WITH PUY LENTILS
*Bottom Left:* PRAWN AND FENNEL RISOTTO

# BRILL WITH WILD MUSHROOM SAUCE

*Serves 4*

Dried ceps add a wonderful depth of flavour to this dish. They are expensive, but you only need a small amount.

| | |
|---|---|
| 15 g/½ oz dried ceps | 2 brill or lemon sole, |
| 150 ml/¼ pint boiling water | filleted |
| 50 ml/2 fl oz brandy | 50 g/2 oz unsalted butter, |
| 150 ml/¼ pint vegetable stock | softened |
| 4 tbsp olive oil | 1 tbsp chopped fresh parsley |
| 2 shallots, chopped | Salt and pepper |
| 225 g/8 oz mixed wild | |
| mushrooms, (e.g. chanterelles, | |
| ceps, blewits, oyster) | |

Soak the dried ceps in the boiling water for 30 minutes. Strain, reserving the liquid, and chop the ceps.

Place the reserved mushroom stock, brandy, and vegetable stock in a pan. Bring to the boil, and simmer to reduce until only about 150 ml/¼ pint remains.

Heat half the oil in a frying pan, and fry the shallots for 3 minutes. Add the soaked and fresh mushrooms, and stir-fry for 5 minutes. Cover and keep warm.

Heat the grill, brush the brill or sole fillets with the remaining oil, and grill for 5-6 minutes until cooked.

Meanwhile, bring the reduced stock to a rolling boil. Whisk in the butter, a little at a time, until the sauce is thickened and glossy.

Transfer the fish to warmed plates, spoon over the mushrooms, and pour over the sauce. Sprinkle with parsley and serve at once.

# FILLET OF TURBOT WITH BRAISED LEEKS

*Serves 4*

Turbot is an expensive fish, but its delicate flavour works well with the leeks. Brill makes a good substitute.

| | |
|---|---|
| 450 g/1 lb baby leeks, | 4 tbsp dry sherry |
| trimmed | 2 tbsp chopped fresh chervil |
| 25 g/1 oz butter | Salt and pepper |
| 2 shallots, quartered | 4 small turbot fillets |
| 2 tsp yellow mustard seeds | 1 tbsp olive oil |

Cut the leeks into thin slices. Melt the butter in a pan, add the shallots and mustard seeds, and fry for 3 minutes. Add the leeks, and fry for a further 3 minutes.

Add the sherry, cover and braise over a low heat for 5-8 minutes until the leeks are tender. Stir in the chervil, and season to taste.

Meanwhile, preheat the grill. Wash the turbot fillets, and pat dry. Brush with a little oil, and place under the grill for 6-8 minutes until cooked through.

Serve the turbot on a bed of braised leeks, with new potatoes and baby carrots.

*Top:* BRILL WITH WILD MUSHROOM SAUCE
*Bottom:* FILLET OF TURBOT WITH BRAISED LEEKS

# MONKFISH WITH PEARS

*Serves 4*

The pears combine surprisingly well
with the monkfish to make an unusual, but
satisfying dish.

≈

| | |
|---|---|
| 4 tbsp walnut oil | 150 ml/¼ pint dry cider or |
| 1 red onion, sliced | unsweetened apple juice |
| 1 garlic clove, crushed | 150 ml/¼ pint vegetable stock |
| 2 tsp chopped fresh sage | 1 tbsp wholegrain mustard |
| 1 tsp fennel seeds | 25 g/1 oz unsalted butter |
| 2 x 450 g/1 lb monkfish | 2 ripe pears, cored and |
| tails, filleted in half | thickly sliced |
| 1 tbsp Calvados or brandy | |

≈

Preheat the oven to 200°C/400°F/Gas mark 6. Heat the oil in a frying pan, and fry the onions, garlic, sage and fennel seeds for 5 minutes, until golden. Using a slotted spoon, transfer to a roasting pan.

Increase the heat under the frying pan, add the monkfish, and fry for 3-4 minutes until well browned all over. Place in the roasting pan on top of the onion mixture.

Pour the Calvados or brandy into the frying pan, ignite and flame. When the flame dies down, add the cider or apple juice, stock and mustard. Bring to the boil, and add to the roasting pan. Transfer to the oven, and bake for 15 minutes.

After 10 minutes, melt the butter in a clean frying pan, and fry the pears for 3-4 minutes until browned on both sides. Remove from the pan, and keep warm.

Remove the roasting pan from the oven. Strain the juices into the frying pan. Cover the monkfish with foil, and keep warm.

Bring the cooking juices to the boil, and simmer to reduce and thicken slightly. Arrange the onion mixture and pears on a serving dish, top with the monkfish fillets, and pour over the sauce. Serve at once with steamed vegetables and baby new potatoes.

# SALMON WITH POTATO AND ARTICHOKE SALAD

*Serves 4*

The warm potato salad in a luscious artichoke
cream complements the salmon perfectly - a
lovely simple summer dish.

≈

| | |
|---|---|
| 4 x 150 g/5 oz salmon fillets, | 400 g/14 oz can cooked |
| skinned | artichoke hearts, drained |
| 600 ml/1 pint Court Bouillon | Juice of ½ lemon |
| (see pages 6-7) | 2 tbsp chopped fresh dill |
| POTATO SALAD | ½ small garlic clove, crushed |
| 450 g/1 lb new potatoes, | 4 tbsp mayonnaise |
| halved | Salt and pepper |

≈

Wash the fish fillets, and pat dry. Cut each fillet into 3 thick slices or large escalopes and place in a pan. Add the court bouillon, bring to the boil, then remove from the heat and leave for 10 minutes.

Transfer the fish to a plate and allow to cool.

Make the salad: simmer the potatoes in boiling water for 10-12 minutes until cooked. Drain well, and place in a serving bowl.

Place all the remaining ingredients in a blender, and purée to form a fairly smooth sauce. Mix with the potatoes. Serve the salmon and salad at room temperature.

*Top:* SALMON WITH POTATO AND ARTICHOKE SALAD
*Bottom:* MONKFISH WITH PEARS

# INDEX